The
Elements of
Library Research

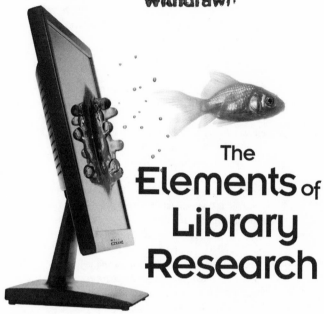

The
Elements of
Library
Research

What Every Student Needs to Know

Mary W. George

PRINCETON UNIVERSITY PRESS
PRINCETON AND OXFORD

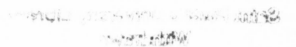

Published by Princeton University Press, 41 William Street, Princeton,
New Jersey 08540
In the United Kingdom: Princeton University Press, 6 Oxford Street, Woodstock,
Oxfordshire OX20 1TW

Library of Congress Cataloging-in-Publication Data
George, Mary W., 1948–
The elements of library research : what every student needs
to know / Mary W. George.
p. cm.
Includes bibliographical references and index.
ISBN 978-0-691-13150-4 (acid-free paper) —
ISBN 978-0-691-13857-2 (pbk. : acid-free paper)
1. Library research—United States.   I. Title.
Z710.G44 2008
025.5'24—dc22   2008013733

British Library Cataloging-in-Publication Data is available
This book has been composed in Minion with Insignia Display
Printed on acid-free paper. ∞

press.princeton.edu
Printed in the United States of America

1   3   5   7   9   10   8   6   4   2

For Emery

Research is formalized curiosity.
It is poking and prying with a purpose.

—Zora Neale Hurston,
Dust Tracks on a Road: An Autobiography

Contents

〜

Preface

〜

This book attempts to answer the questions every student has about conducting college-level library research. For years, I have watched undergraduates approach each new research assignment—whether to write a short essay, review previous work in a field, support a debate position, or gather primary and secondary sources for a long term paper—as if they have never needed information before. Yet I know they have successfully discovered facts and ideas since childhood, so why is every project such a struggle? Technology alone is not to blame: students were puzzled and anxious about how to do library research long before Web searching became everyone's first, and often only, method of information gathering.

I think part of the problem has to do with unfamiliar surroundings and unrealistic expectations. No two libraries are exactly alike. Each has a distinctive book and periodical collection and its own array of electronic resources. People who can quickly orient themselves to other complex places, such as a large shopping mall or a busy airport, somehow have trouble functioning in a strange library, or when presented with a vast array of choices on a computer screen. College faculty assume students are already acquainted with a handful of reference works and that they can find background information and use an online catalog and article database on their own. Many professors have forgotten how daunting it is for a new student to look up a book by its author or title, translate its call number into an actual location, then get to the right shelf in a library with several floors on a campus that may have several libraries.

Students' own expectations about library research are likewise flawed. First, their past experience leads them to conclude that everything worth knowing can be found instantly on the Internet. Second, they believe each research assignment is unique and that there can be no connection between their efforts for a presentation on global warming and their work for a paper on Mozart. Third, they arrive in college convinced that research and writing will be the same activities they engaged in previously, mostly gathering and summarizing sources. And fourth, they can be too proud or embarrassed to seek advice. Separately and together these misconceptions spell trouble.

That trouble is avoidable once students grasp the concepts, components, and logic of the information-seeking process and realize how they can judge and use the sources they discover. This book reveals the elements of library research that experienced researchers take for granted. My aim is to replace anxiety with an understanding of patterns and possibilities—in other words, with a method students can apply to all their work in college and beyond. This advice does not work on its own, but makes sense in the context of real research assignments and with the guidance of faculty and librarians.

My intended audience includes novice researchers in any rigorous academic setting, whether high school or college, who need reliable sources. My ideal readers are curious, eager to explore, and bold about adding their own thoughts to the mix. My greatest hope is that students will learn to adapt the process to all their future inquiries.

∽

I could not have written these chapters without the insights I have gained from the thousands of students I have worked closely with over the years. It has taken me a long time to realize that just because undergraduates have more diverse interests, ask more complex questions, and are more savvy about technology than even a decade ago does not mean they are any more adept at finding good, current information. Every consultation I have had with a student has, in some unfathomable way, helped shape the content of this book. I thank them all.

I owe a debt of gratitude to Kerry Walk and to the past and present instructors in the Princeton Writing Program. She and they have focused my attention on the nature of academic argument and the challenges of introducing that topic to freshmen, intertwined as it must be with the search for, and evaluation of, sources.

Four librarians have inspired and sustained me in this venture: Connie Dunlap, my early mentor at the University of Michigan; Anne Beaubien, also of the University of Michigan; the late Sharon Hogan of the University of Illinois at Chicago; and Tom Kirk of Earlham College. My former Princeton colleague Kevin Barry, now the director of Ohrstrom Library at St. Paul's School in Concord, New Hampshire, was outstandingly supportive during the months I spent drafting and revising this manuscript.

My understanding of the experience of information seeking has come from the pioneering thought of Carol

Kuhlthau of Rutgers University, whose model of the process correlates the researcher's thoughts and feelings with each phase of investigation. She has been my inspiration in more ways than she knows.

I am most grateful to Anne Savarese at Princeton University Press for understanding my intent, for her wise editorial advice, and for her instant reply to my e-mail query asking if the Press would be interested in this topic. No author could wish for more.

Finally, and most especially, I want to thank my husband, Emery George, for his quiet encouragement and daily example as an untiring researcher, scholar, author, and teacher.

The
Elements of
Library Research

1

Introduction to Research as Inquiry

Let me explain what this little book is and why I am writing it. It is not a guide to whipping up successful research papers from dribs and drabs of information. Nor is it a set of commandments or a list of random reference works. It is about the interplay of ideas (yours) with sources (from outside yourself) and about the nature and discovery of those sources. I want to persuade you, as a serious but uncertain student, that library research is not a mystery or a lucky dodge, but an investigation you control from start to finish, even though you cannot usually tell *what* sources you will discover. Like its twin, scientific experiment, library research is a form of structured inquiry with specific tools, rules, and techniques. Also like its twin, it is unpredictable, sometimes frustrating, but ultimately rewarding as you examine your findings, then add your own insights to make a compelling case. As a bonus, when you share your work—whether through writing, speaking, or technology—addressing one person or a wide audience, *you* create a new source, extending the cycle. There is no more fulfilling intellectual experience.

What do I mean by *student* and *library* in the previous paragraph? I want to reach anyone who feels anxious—or downright scared—when facing a task that involves seeking and weighing information. You may be starting your first research paper, your n^{th} term project, even your doctoral dissertation: if you worry that you are not going to find enough of the "right stuff," then the ideas and suggestions in this book will put you at ease and back in charge. Each time you work through the library research process, regardless of how different your aim or subject is from your previous efforts, you will become more fluent. Soon you will see how to modify the method and what alternatives exist if you are missing a key fact or suspect that a source cannot be trusted. As with any other complex activity, repetition with variations will lead first to mastery, then to creativity.

Novices often think that unless they have a gigantic university library at their disposal, they will fail to find all the sources they need. Not so. A bigger collection is not necessarily a better one for a specific research project. Not only are tens of millions of reputable sources of all sorts now in digital form as licensed databases or free on the Web, but libraries can often obtain material from elsewhere within a few days. Unless and until you come up short in the nearby collections available to you—typically your school's own library and your local public library—I urge you not to worry. But if you do conclude that you need more sources, speak with both your instructor (assuming you are doing a course-related research project) and a reference librarian about what you can do.

Likewise, do not assume dire consequences if your library does not have all the reference works and databases I mention. I name these titles simply as examples, not as necessary resources for everyone. Once you understand what each type of tool does, you can figure out—on your own or by asking—what your library has to offer for the job.

Moving from the Known to the New

When you are familiar with an activity because you have done it flawlessly in the past, then you do not give it much time or thought or emotion. Why would you, unless the outcome is especially significant, such as earning a high grade on a math exam tomorrow so that you can take calculus next term?

But if an activity is new to you—if it is familiar but a lot more complex than anything you have done in the past, if factors such as the setting or criteria for success are strange—then you will inevitably be unsure, anxious, and probably tempted to avoid the experience. Think about the first time you needed to figure out a big city's public transportation system on your own, so that you could travel from point A to point B within an hour. It was stressful—right?—even if all the maps and signs were in English. Now imagine the first time you got behind the wheel of a car, presumably after learning dozens of rules and cautions in a driver's education class. My guess is that although you felt somewhat uncertain about what to do and the order to do it in, you were so eager to get your permit that you remember the event as a stimulating rather than a harrowing experience.

These scenarios illustrate the range of research projects you will encounter in college and beyond, some completely foreign to you and others for which you have some background or experience. The trait they share is the hunt for "what's out there," a favorite phrase of teachers everywhere.

In the following sections I cover the purposes of research in general, the varieties of research, and the ways researchers communicate their findings. I start this way because I want to convince you that the library research process is part of a larger universe of inquiry. If you can identify the facets of any research study you encounter, and figure out how someone designed it (or could have designed it better), then you will be much readier for college-level research than most students, whether in a library or a laboratory. As you read the next few pages, keep in mind that your professors live and breathe these issues as they go about the business of creating new knowledge in their fields.

Reasons for Research

Before we examine the varieties and characteristics of research, we should consider why anyone does formal research in the first place. Here is a list of research goals I encounter frequently on a university campus, but they occur in other settings as well, such as in business, government, and professional organizations. Research serves to

1. Reveal the cause or causes of a phenomenon
2. Resolve an anomaly (something that doesn't make sense)
3. Test a hypothesis or develop a theory
4. Verify or replicate someone else's findings
5. Determine what a new instrument or technique can do
6. Adapt methods or results from one field to another
7. Observe or record an event as it occurs
8. Reproduce conditions from the past in the present
9. Understand human motivations for actions
10. Isolate factors and their interrelationships in a complex system
11. Predict or influence individual or group behavior
12. Improve the quality of life across cultures and populations
13. Analyze the components of a creative work

No doubt you can supply examples of each of these research incentives from your own reading and experience. I suggest you keep track of additional ones you come across from now on. My point is that although a researcher's intent helps determine the specific methods he or she will use, all researchers share a deep, universal aim: to discover the truth about something that intrigues them.

Varieties of Research

Most people think about research in large categories labeled with the field of the researcher or the course that requires a research project. For instance, you might refer to *historical research, scientific research, textual research,* or *sociological research.* These phrases suffice for general communication about what is meant, and they are the ones you see and hear in the media. They are not, however, precise as to the *way* someone tackles a research problem. The following chart lists some, but by no means all, of the common approaches to investigation used in research projects (also frequently called research studies), with brief descriptions. I don't dwell on any of them except the first—which is, after all, what this book is about. I simply want to lay out the cards so you will see how diverse the deck of inquiry is. The forms of research toward the top of the chart are the ones you are most likely to encounter during your first two years of college.

These methods overlap in real life—in fact, it's unusual for a given project *not* to involve more than one of them. Furthermore, the qualitative, quantitative, and empirical approaches are umbrella terms that can be applied to other methods as well. For now, just be alert to this variety.

Research Method	Characteristics and Examples
Library	Involves identifying and locating sources that provide factual information or personal/expert opinion on a research question; necessary component of every other research method at some point
Experimental	Takes place in a dedicated environment, typically a laboratory, and involves specific equipment and procedural steps; molecular biological research to decode a species' genome is an example
Explicatory	Entails a careful, close, and focused examination of a single major text, or of evidence surrounding a single complex event, in an attempt to understand one or more aspects of it—for instance, why a poem is pleasing, or the probable causes of an event
Field	Occurs wherever the phenomenon under study exists, meaning the researcher goes to that location; archaeological excavation is one type
Observational	Takes place either in a laboratory or in the field, but entails capturing an exact record of some behavior (of either animate or inanimate objects); child psychologists who watch infants interact do this sort of research. Note that researchers may be observers or participants in the phenomenon they are studying, as when an anthropologist lives in a remote village to record the language used by people during religious ceremonies

Research Method	Characteristics and Examples
Interview	Includes any sort of conversation that addresses a specific experience or issue about which the interviewee is knowledgeable, involves questions prepared in advance, and is recorded in its entirety; oral history, for instance
Survey	Poses a series of questions to a group of people (usually a sample) with specific responses for individuals to choose from; usually captures demographic and socioeconomic information as well, to correlate with the responses; written questionnaires and telephone opinion polls are examples
Longitudinal	Follows a phenomenon over time; often used in educational or medical studies where the individuals in a group are periodically reexamined at specific intervals over many years
Archival	Involves the researcher in a close study of original documents—typically collected and retained by governments, organizations, or families—that exist in a unique location; genealogical research is a case in point
Qualitative	Designates any research whose results are captured in words, images, or nonnumeric symbols; for instance, research on dreams
Quantitative	Describes any approach where the phenomenon under study is captured via measurement and expressed in numbers that can be analyzed; opposite of qualitative research; econometric research on the international oil trade is an example

(continued)

Research Method	Characteristics and Examples
Empirical	Refers to studies using experiment or observation to test the validity of a phenomenon; less rigorously, refers to knowledge derived from experience, as when people assert that, based on empirical evidence, the sun will rise tomorrow morning
Theoretical	Entails speculation on the part of the researcher, and is usually based on the findings of other kinds of studies, in an attempt to account for or predict the behavior of a phenomenon; Einstein's work is a case in point

How Researchers Share Their Findings

You can think of these and other research methods as the engine of the new-knowledge-creation process, the necessary transformative stage between the researcher's curiosity and conclusions. Before you can appreciate those conclusions or take part in the process itself, you should be aware of the various ways researchers convey their results and interpretations to other experts and to the general public.

Here is yet another list, this time of how and where researchers most commonly communicate. Since most of these channels are familiar or self-explanatory, I keep my elaboration to a minimum. The product of research can be

1. A report in the form of a peer-reviewed article in a scholarly journal
2. An announcement in the form of a press release, interview, or story written by a journalist for a news publication or popular periodical
3. A book (also called a monograph when it is devoted to a single, complex topic)
4. A chapter in a collection of essays addressing the same or related themes
5. A presentation at a conference, sometimes later published in a proceedings volume or as a journal article
6. A master's thesis or doctoral dissertation, which may later be revised and issued as a book
7. A memoir or autobiography, typically by a senior scholar reflecting on his or her research career and appearing in journal article, chapter, or book format
8. A comment on another researcher's work, such as a letter to the editor or a book review, published in a newspaper or periodical
9. Nonprint media such as e-mail, listserv postings, blogs, personal Web pages, filmed documentaries, or broadcast interviews on radio or television
10. An overview or synthesis in an encyclopedia article or college textbook
11. Classroom teaching, conversations with colleagues, and student advising, types of communication that are seldom published but may well be captured and preserved as lecture notes, in footnotes, or in the acknowledgments of books or journal articles

In the course of your college education, you will read about each of these forms of communication. You will likely observe your professors engage in or allude to them as well.

Peer Review

This is an essential activity in the world of learning. In its more general sense, peer review means that specialists on a topic have a duty to evaluate the work of others in the same area of expertise—just as those with experience in the professions serve as gatekeepers for their field. In its narrower sense, a peer-reviewed article is one that scholars in a discipline have judged to be worthwhile *before* it is published in a journal, thus assuring that poor research and weak arguments never see the light of day.

Literature Review

A standard outcome of research is a literature review (also called a *research review* or a *review of the literature*). This is a paragraph, section, or entire chapter—depending on the nature and length of the publication—in which the author identifies and comments on previous attempts to answer the same, or related, research questions. Although you may never be asked to include a formal research review in anything you write in college, you will most definitely be expected to do research reviews for various projects, mainly to back up your own ideas and arguments, but also to prove to your teachers that you can identify and evaluate relevant sources.

Don't be misled by the phrases *literature review* or *review of the literature.* They refer to a summary of related research in *any* field. The terms are not limited to the novels, poems, or plays you read in an English course. So you may well come across a literature review on AIDS-related infant mortality in a journal article by medical researchers describing their study of the disease in newborns.

Practice Critical Thinking

Create a dedicated computer file, notebook, or folder where you keep track of interesting research projects you encounter. Include where and how you came across the information, so that you can get back to it in the future. A good method is to regularly examine current issues, either online or in print at your library, of periodicals that carry what I call breakthrough stories: for example, any of the major news magazines (*Newsweek, Time, U.S. News & World Report*); the science section of a daily newspaper; or publications like *Nature, Psychology Today, Science,* or *Scientific American.* In each issue, look at the table of contents and choose the article that most intrigues you. Read it thoroughly and make notes about the questions the researchers address, the methods they use, and how they describe the results of their study. If other ideas occur to you—for instance, if you've read an article about how honeybees communicate and you wonder whether the same conclusions apply to wasps—write those down too, so you will get in the habit of thinking critically about the work of others. Be sure to record the bibliographic details of the article: author(s), title of the article, name of the publication, date, and page(s). If you prefer, you can print out or photocopy the article, write the bibliographic details on the copy (if they are not already present), and put your own comments in the margins.

The rest of this book guides you through the process of identifying sources for your own research projects. For now just realize that everyone starting a complex inquiry needs to discover two things: as much background information as possible on their topic of interest; and the research, conclusions, and opinions of others who have examined the same topic and asked similar questions about it. Even a genius must start from the work of earlier thinkers, a truth symbolized by the image of Sir Isaac Newton (1642–1727) seeing farther because, as he is reputed to have said, he stood on the shoulders of giants—that is, of his own predecessors.

From Here Forward

The next chapter of this book expands on the idea of library research as inquiry and recommends an efficient, effective way to plan your investigation *before* you start to uncover evidence. To do this, it offers a diagram of the library research process, three key definitions, and several suggestions for choosing a congenial research topic. It also raises the gnarly matter of plagiarism and introduces Mary's Maxims, a few friendly injunctions to all library researchers, which I intersperse throughout the book. The purpose of these maxims is to lower your anxiety and raise your expectations—and, I hope, your enjoyment—as you conduct library research in any setting.

Chapter 3 focuses on a basic, and versatile, library research strategy and the tools you need to wield at each stage. I concentrate on the characteristics of each kind of reference work and give examples, recognizing that your own library may well have different resources that perform the same functions.

Chapter 4 addresses practical issues everyone confronts in the course of research. I describe in detail the known-item and concept approaches for identifying sources and the two complementary variations of the latter, keyword and subject searching. I also go over search logic, the nontrivial matter of locating and obtaining items, and some other techniques for discovering evidence.

Chapter 5 considers ways to evaluate sources and discusses the dynamism of inquiry—that is, the ever-shifting relationship among research questions, findings, and insight. Although this is emphatically not a composition textbook, I offer a few words about developing an argument, dealing with obstacles in the writing process, and documenting all the pertinent evidence. This final chapter reiterates a serious message I address at several points in the book: avoiding plagiarism. To conclude, I extract the principles and techniques covered earlier and suggest how, with a bit of tailoring, you can extrapolate them from one inquiry to the next—across time, place, and topics, as you move through your education and daily life.

2

From Research Assignment
to Research Plan

Every living thing gathers information continuously in order to survive. That information comes from both the environment and within the organism itself, arriving without conscious activity. Then there is the intentional information seeking we do constantly as human beings in the course of our daily personal, social, and work lives. Suppose you have a doubt about a fact, a sequence, or a policy, for instance, "I don't know where the nearest ABC store is located, if they allow exchanges of merchandise purchased elsewhere, or if they will refund the purchase price in cash or give me store credit." So, almost without thinking, you search their Web site, make a phone call, check a recent newspaper ad—whatever you judge will be the most effective, quickest way to answer your question. It's second nature.

Moving from second-nature reasoning and behavior in everyday life to similar reasoning and behavior in one's academic or professional life should be seamless and painless. But somehow it's not. Confronted with a typical array of factors—motivation (need or curiosity), elements (givens and unknowns), and resources (time available, technologies, tools)—most people tend to panic and falter in a formal setting such as a class- or work-related project imposed by an authority figure. This is a variant of the fight-or-flight instinct, the urge to understand versus the urge to duck. Since the point of education is to learn and apply, it follows that ducking is not an option, whereas understanding is. Any discomfort you might feel with library research is perfectly normal—but so is your innate ability to master the tools and process.

The Nature of Research Projects

I define a research project as any task that requires, or would benefit from, factual information or opinions you do not already have. If you think of research projects as games—not as spectator sports or pastimes, but as activities that demand a commitment to both mental and physical exertion—then it's easier to grasp their variety. Each kind of research project has its own goals, rules, boundaries, tactics, traditions, and ways of keeping score. Some are solitary, while others involve a team effort with each player assuming a necessary role.

There are research projects you can accomplish based on your own prior experience or by following the advice of others. There are those that respond to ordinary logic, although you still need to know what moves are allowed. Yet others entail special skills or methods you can master only with practice. As with games, research projects are most rewarding if you have good coaches—teachers, advisors, librarians, current or retired practitioners, eyewitnesses— and if you take the time to observe how pros face similar challenges. Whatever their characteristics, all research projects require imagination and the ability to turn an assignment into an investigation, a topic into an inquiry.

You may well wonder about good (or bad) luck as a factor in research projects, as it is in games and life generally. Only the most arrogant researcher would deny the importance of luck, but it is usually disguised in formal contexts with words like *serendipity* or *sample contamination*. Just remember that the unexpected will happen, sooner or later. Wise researchers will quickly spot an opportunity or a problem and will adjust their methods and conclusions accordingly.

The analogy between games and research projects is not perfect. The key difference between the two pursuits is that games have real or implied opponents, whereas research projects are efforts to understand something new (at least to you, the researcher). It follows that the criteria for success are also different. You win a game by achieving the best score or the fastest time. You succeed at a research project when you have identified, described, and discussed the significance of something you did not know before.

Where We're Headed: A Map

The library research process per se has nine stages, indicated by the shaded area in figure 2.1. To elaborate slightly, they are (1) choosing a general topic, (2) engaging your imagination, (3) highlighting one or more research questions as a result of brainstorming about your topic, (4) developing a research plan or strategy, (5) consulting reference tools and searching databases, (6) identifying and obtaining sources, (7) evaluating sources in the light of your research questions, (8) experiencing an insight based on reflection, and (9) crafting a thesis statement based on your insight. Each stage requires mental effort and agility, but the process is no more challenging than other sequential activities you engage in. You will be a proficient researcher when you can move comfortably through all nine stages and can anticipate and surmount difficulties along the way.

The steps outside the shaded area in figure 2.1 (first your motivation or assignment, then, toward the end, your argument and outline, and finally drafting and revising your presentation) are also part of the process. I discuss each in its place, but in less detail than the central elements.

What about *imagination* and *insight,* the two words I've emphasized in figure 2.1? Researchers must allow time, starting early in the process, to consider their work from all angles, in other words, to speculate and to dream about it. That is what I mean by imagination, when the conscious mind buddies up with the unconscious mind to help solve a research problem. You cannot force imagination to kick in, but you can schedule intervals for the reflection that is likely to promote it. As for insight, researchers can never predict when in the process they will have what is widely called the "Aha!" moment, the intuitive instant when they see a solution to their investigation. I put insight between the evaluation and thesis steps because that's where I usually experience it, but it can come at any point.

One more point about this flowchart: it's rarely linear in real life. Typically some of the stages will overlap, and seasoned researchers will tell you that occasionally they step aside to explore another angle, pause briefly, or even double back to a previous point. It might be best to envision the process as a spiral ramp or as a flexible chain of elastic links where the whole can expand or contract or loop around itself, depending on the complexity of the inquiry and the energy you apply to it.

Core Definitions

Before we go any further, let me elaborate on three words that are crucial in this book: the verb *to find* and the nouns *source* and *tool.* These are terms we all use daily in a variety

MARY'S MAXIM #1:
Imagination and Insight are Inseparable

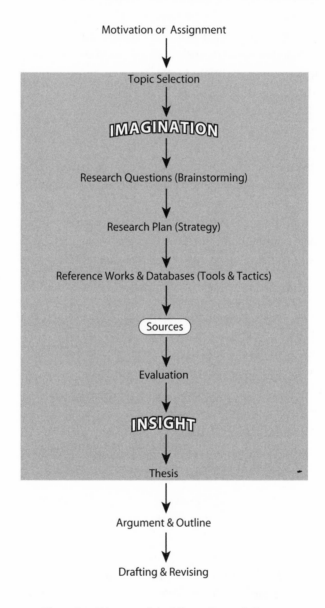

Motivation or Assignment

Topic Selection

IMAGINATION

Research Questions (Brainstorming)

Research Plan (Strategy)

Reference Works & Databases (Tools & Tactics)

Sources

Evaluation

INSIGHT

Thesis

Argument & Outline

Drafting & Revising

Figure 2.1: Diagram of the Library Research Process

of contexts, but as I explain the library research process, I mean them in a more restricted sense. *To find* (which does not appear in figure 2.1) is an imprecise expression that can mean *to discover facts about, to identify the existence of, to locate, to obtain,* or (often) several of these actions at once. When you say to me—or to any reference librarian—"I can't find enough information on X," you will trigger a friendly interrogation as I probe to determine more precisely what you wish to accomplish and what you have already tried. Please don't think I am prying or that I want to embarrass you; I am trying to understand your project so I can make the most helpful suggestions. This is the same technique you expect when you deal with any professional. If a doctor, lawyer, accountant, or interior designer did not ask you questions at the start of a conversation on a complex matter, but just told you what to do in a perfunctory tone, you would be skeptical about his or her competence and rightly offended. The same is true when you approach a reference librarian, whether in person, electronically, or by phone. I promise to be as clear as possible throughout this book about what sense(s) of *to find* I intend every time I use that verb.

By *source* I always mean the evidence that supplies at least a partial answer to your inquiry, either supporting your hunches or contradicting them. Sources come in an infinite variety of physical shapes (including, not surprisingly, human ones) and we will look at several common types later in this chapter. But beyond packaging, the defining feature of a "good source" is that it will convey information—whether fact, observation, opinion, or some combination of those— that relates to your work *and that you must evaluate* in the light of both other sources and your own insights as your research proceeds. Put another way, what makes a source good rather than neutral is the addition of your own judg-

What Is a Librarian?

For the record, college and university librarians have at least one graduate degree: a master's in information science from one of more than fifty universities in the United States and Canada with an accredited program in the field. Most librarians on any campus will have other advanced degrees as well, so you may well confer with an economics librarian who has an MBA, a life sciences librarian who holds an MS in biochemistry, or a foreign language specialist librarian with a PhD in Spanish. Librarians in other settings—high schools, public libraries, and law firms, for instance—also have graduate degrees or certifications appropriate to their work. Just as not everyone who works with patients in a hospital is a physician, not everyone who helps you in a library is a librarian. Modern academic libraries have employees with many backgrounds, talents, and duties. You can generally assume, however, that you will get research assistance from a highly trained and experienced professional.

ment. Even when you believe a source is weak or wrong, you can still use it to argue *against,* while presenting your own ideas and other sources to back them up.

By *tool* I always mean anything that either encapsulates common knowledge or points you to a source. For instance, a dictionary defines words and their usage; a library's catalog indicates what books and other materials you will find (locate) in its collection; an encyclopedia article both summarizes information on a topic and offers a few good sources in a list of further readings. Think of a tool as the appropriate utensil for the job at hand. You would no more use a dictionary to get a telephone number than you would use a strainer to serve broth.

The three major categories of tools essential to the library research process are what I call *fact tools* (like a dictionary), *finding tools* (like a library catalog), and *hybrid tools* (like an encyclopedia). I consider these in detail in chapter 3.

Familiarities

You will probably be struck by the similarity between the steps in figure 2.1 and the standard depiction of the scientific method described in any science textbook—or, for that matter, the list of research methods in chapter 1. The resemblance should be no surprise: all forms of research involve a transition from ignorance to knowledge through the action of human thought on evidence. What is distinctive about library research—and I always include archival research in that phrase—is that the evidence has already been captured and stored. Your job as researcher is to discover the evidence, an effort that can require as many as five steps: (1) identifying sources that seem relevant, (2) determining where they are located, (3) obtaining them, (4) evaluating them for the project at hand, and (5) incorporating them into your argument or presentation. Thanks to digital and Web technology, you will often be able to complete the first four actions simultaneously, but in chapters 4 and 5 I discuss the steps separately so you will know how to do things the old-fashioned way when necessary. For now, just be aware that **the logic of the library research process is the movement from what exists to what is worth using.**

As you know, the catalyst in the scientific method is either a theory or an observation that leads to a hypothesis—otherwise known as a thoughtful guess that someone can test using standard procedures. Both approaches require curiosity about what is happening in the natural world and why. Scientific curiosity cannot be satisfied in one effort, however. Other researchers must be able to replicate any test and confirm the results, which (and this is a critical matter) must be both reliable and valid indicators of the phenomenon in question.

Research in the social sciences proceeds in a similar way, but because those fields concern aspects of human nature rather than of physical or biological nature, practitioners use different methods and instruments to test their hypotheses and to reproduce the work of others. In the humanities, strict scientific method yields to different approaches to satisfy curiosity and extend knowledge. Instead of experts asking one another, "Can you find what I found?" as in the sciences and social sciences, humanities scholars ask, "Do you see what I see?" about a text, an image, a musical composition, or a performance. Regardless of discipline or method, all researchers strive to be systematic and to challenge their peers about the meaning and significance of their interests. Often their challenges are mysterious (at least to the layperson), self-centered, or quarrelsome, but that is a story for others to tell.

I draw these distinctions because the library research process has many of the information-seeking patterns already familiar to you. Furthermore, library research is an integral part of inquiry in any field, allowing researchers to determine what related work has already been done and how experts have assessed it. (A literature review, described in chapter 1, is simply a summary of the prior work and interpretations of it.) In short, the library research process is similar in nature to other forms of inquiry. It is an investigation involving accepted facts, unknowns, speculation, logical procedures rigorously applied, verification, evaluation, repetition, and ultimately an interpretation of findings that extends understanding. What makes the library research process unique, and why you need to start practicing it early and often in your life, is that it is fundamental to every other way people seek knowledge, a technique as essential as sautéing is for an aspiring chef.

The Experience of Research

Let's pause to face an issue I bet neither you nor any of your instructors has ever addressed: library research, done well, is a challenge that involves thinking, acting, and uncertainty. This book suggests ways of thinking about research problems and ways of acting to obtain information. But that's just two-thirds of the game. The other third, equally important, is your emotional state as you work through the often-complex process of discovering sources related to your assignment, evaluating your finds in the light of your own ideas, and—often, but not always—repeating or adding steps in the research process as your focus sharpens.

What I'm describing is a fluctuating wave of anxiety that you will inevitably experience in the course of *every* research project. Feeling uneasy, doubtful, or overwhelmed about your investigation is not just a common, but an essential, part of human experience, the labor pains that lead from ignorance to accomplishment. I think of the "research blues" as the price each of us must pay in advance for the moments of insight and creativity that follow. Does nervous tension decrease with experience? Not much, because each research project you undertake, even in the same field at a more advanced level, still starts at the edge of what seems like a bottomless pit of unknowns. The good news is that, over time, your fears of failure and inadequacy will become less distracting as your confidence, based on past success, slowly rises.

In sum, you should expect to feel bewildered or discouraged at least once during your research. One remedy, which should be no surprise, is to take a brief respite from your work—while avoiding the temptation to abandon it in despair. Later on, I suggest various ways to move beyond any impasses you encounter.

Practical Matters: Getting Comfortable with Spaces (Physical and Virtual)

Before you begin any complex task, it is wise to check out your surroundings. Infants, young children, and animals all do this instinctively, exploring their environment for clues to survival. But the older humans get, the more self-assured they become, an attitude that can lead to discovery and creativity—or to dangerous behavior. We all recognize the pros and cons of risk-taking in life, and the necessity at times to make quick decisions without adequate information, but there is seldom a valid reason to tackle a course-related library research project on the fly.

Ironically, orientation is the step most researchers skip, assuming that all physical libraries and all library Web sites are more or less identical. But if you do not dedicate a few minutes to reconnoiter each new library building you encounter, along with its corresponding home page, you will lose not only time but also momentum in your research. Worse yet, you will lose confidence. At some unconscious level, anxiety will set in, eventually breeding such side effects as fear of library research, irritation, defensiveness, mood swings, procrastination, grab-and-go Internet surfing, and—I hesitate to name this—plagiarism, or a serious temptation to it. To forestall these dire consequences, here are two basic checklists of information you should acquaint yourself with on your first visit to any library building and to any library Web site.

SELF-ORIENTATION CHECKLIST FOR ANY LIBRARY BUILDING

This should take half an hour or less, thirty minutes you will never regret. (Hint: It's more fun to explore with a friend or two.)

- ❑ Where are all the entrances? What is the security method? Is it electronic, or is staff stationed near the exits or on patrol? Do you need to show an identification card or special pass on the way in?
- ❑ Where, how, and when can you check out materials? If you have borrowing privileges, find out whether you need to register or activate your card. If so, do it now.
- ❑ Where are there public computer clusters? Do those machines run the Mac or the Windows operating system? Do you see printers and scanners nearby and, if so, can you tell whether there is a per page charge for using them? Does the library lend or rent laptops to students?
- ❑ Where can you get assistance with your research? Where can you ask directional and how-to questions, get advice on searching the catalog and databases, or speak with a librarian?
- ❑ What is the general arrangement of the collection? Specifically, what kinds of materials are shelved on each floor? Whether or not there are handouts or posted signs that make this clear, *take a trip*. Start on the top floor—or bottom, if you prefer—and scout around.

Pay attention not only to which subjects occupy each level but also to ambient spaces, such as group study rooms, areas with informal seating, lockers, and (not least!) the location of restrooms and water fountains. Help yourself to a printed floor plan, if there is one, and mark on it two or three places where you see tables or desks in quiet areas where you can settle in to do serious reading, studying, or writing.

❑ If you will be bringing your own laptop to the library, check whether these quiet areas have a wireless signal (or Internet jacks) and electrical outlets.

❑ Note the location of elevators, stairways, and emergency exit doors. While you are sleuthing, look for important research places, such as special collections, the reference room, new book displays, exhibition areas, current periodicals and newspapers, bound (older) periodicals, the reserve desk, video and music listening facilities, an auditorium or classrooms, staff and faculty offices, and photocopiers. If there is a café or vending area, find that too.

As you explore the environs and note the services and facilities in the building, be sure to pick up any brochures or library newsletters, especially if they describe services or "treasures" you were unaware of. (Remember: expert staff members are treasures too!) If you are puzzled by anything you see—or don't see—then *ask* someone for clarification before you leave.

SELF-ORIENTATION CHECKLIST FOR ANY LIBRARY WEB SITE

You can, of course, examine a library's Web site from anywhere, but if you have the time, I recommend that you do this while you are still *in* the building. That way, if you are curious about something, you can speak with a staff member on the spot.

❑   Is there a single home page for the library? How do you navigate there from the institution's home page? (Hint: If the library is not a link on a college or university home page, try looking under headings such as "Academics" or "Research" or "Services.")

❑   Where is the link to the library catalog? Does the catalog have a distinctive name, such as TigerCat or InfoLink? (You might also encounter the term *opac,* an acronym for the clunky phrase *online public access catalog.*) See if you can tell whether the catalog includes items from all campus or branch libraries—this is typically the case—or whether there are separate catalogs, for instance, for the life sciences, which may happen if your university has a medical school. Conversely, does the catalog represent the library holdings of more than one institution? Some libraries belong to a consortium and share one catalog. This is a great convenience, as long as you recognize that some sources you identify will not be on the shelf in your local library, but may require delivery on request from a distance.

❑   Where are the links to various types of electronic resources, such as encyclopedias, dictionaries, handbooks, databases listing periodical or newspaper articles, and whole digitized books? How are these links organized? Can you quickly tell how to connect to these resources from off campus? Do you see links to other libraries' Web sites you might want at some point, such as those of nearby college and public libraries?

❑   How can you use the library's Web pages to contact a
     staff member? What forms of communication—for
     example, reference help via e-mail or a Web form, in-
     stant messaging, walk-in service, telephone numbers—
     are available and when? Is there a staff list organized by
     discipline or responsibility so that you can determine
     who is the library's expert on what?

❑   Can you easily determine library hours and policies,
     such as whether you can renew items without bringing
     them back to the building?

❑   What research guides, tutorials, or navigational hand-
     outs are available online?

As soon as you can, bookmark the library's home page on
your own computer. While you're at it, also bookmark (and
similarly explore) the home pages of the public library and
of any neighboring college's library so that these links will be
handy when you want them.

Launching a Library Research Project

You've gathered by now that research of all sorts, including
library research, is a serious form of investigation. Through a
series of more or less standard procedures, it leads you from
what you imperfectly know to a clearer view of your subject. Unless you conduct research simply to satisfy your own
curiosity, you will also need to interpret what you discover
and explain your work and reasoning to an audience. Remember that academic research is not over until it's com-
municated.

If your incentive for library research is a class assignment,
the next maxim will help you get started.

⤳ MARY'S MAXIM #2: BE SURE YOU
UNDERSTAND THE ASSIGNMENT

Questions you need clear answers to at the start of your research include

- How does it relate to the rest of your course work?
- What guidelines or restrictions are there for your choice of topic?
- Are there any interim deadlines before the entire project is due?
- Can you get feedback on an outline or draft from your instructor?
- What counts toward your grade for the research project?

In addition, if the project will result in a written paper, you need to know

- Who will be reading your paper?
- How long should it be (minimum and maximum word or page count)?
- What quantity and variety of sources should you aim for?
- What bibliographic style should you use? In a nutshell, this is how your teacher expects your final paper to *look*, in particular the appearance of your notes and your list of works cited—aka your bibliography. This may seem like a superficial matter, but I assure you it is not. You can refer to the bibliography in this book for a list of the most common bibliographic styles, but usually either your professor or your academic department will specify which one you should follow.
- Can you see another student's well-researched, well-written, and well-documented paper, based on the same assignment, from an earlier term?

Alternatively, if the project will culminate in an oral presentation, you should learn

- Who will be your audience?
- How long will you have to speak, and where?
- Should you read your text, talk from notes, or speak from memory?
- What sort of handout or projections does your teacher recommend?
- Will you also need to turn in a written version of your talk?

Need a Topic?

I smile whenever I hear novice researchers—and this includes graduate students beginning their dissertations—say, "I'm looking for a topic that . . ." or "I haven't found a topic yet" or "I have a topic, but I'm afraid it's too broad (or narrow)." The verbs *to look, to find,* and *to have* in this context are certainly correct English, but the image they convey amuses me. In my mind's eye I see these speakers on hands and knees peering and poking underneath a huge toadstool in a dense forest, exactly like storybook elves, trying to discover a tasty topic (or at least a satisfactory one) that must certainly be hiding in the underbrush. When they locate such a thing, they snatch it without scoping out the area to see if a juicier topic may be in full view nearby. Then they glance around furtively to make sure no one was watching, and dash home with what they assume is a prize. Their problem is then how to prepare the topic for company, often in the absence of time, a tested recipe, or the necessary ingredients.

But if you don't find a topic on the ground, then where do you get one? Following are five methods I recommend. In words of one syllable they are *ask, read, browse, look,* and *link.* I urge you to try each of them (for different research assignments) before you graduate. My main advice is to **choose something that interests you**—if not forever, then at least for the duration of the project. If nothing about ecology grabs your attention, for example, you might decide to look at political debates on hunting and fishing in national parks, an approach that may well satisfy both your curiosity and the assignment.

◥ MARY'S MAXIM #3: WHEN PICKING
A TOPIC, LIKE IT OR LEAVE IT OR TWEAK IT

Topic Selection Method 1: Ask

Some students take the bold and not unreasonable approach of asking their instructor to suggest "a good topic" along with a way of addressing it. The advantage of this tactic is that your instructor presumably is interested in whatever she recommends (and knows your strengths and weaknesses as well as those of the library's collection), so that if you do a good job of research, thinking, and presentation, the result will engage and please her. But requesting a topic also has drawbacks. You may not like the advice you get, even after you spend time trying to explore the topic's contours and meanings. That will put you in the awkward position of either pretending you care about the topic (a ruse your instructor is bound to recognize) or abandoning it late in the game (causing you to worry about angering her). Maybe your instructor is—or believes herself to be—an expert on the topic who offers the same idea to every student who asks. Working with an expert makes some students uneasy because they decide they can never measure up to Professor Big Name's reputation. My advice: either ignore her fame or seek and relish her wisdom. If you choose the latter, however, do it sincerely and because you want to learn. Remember that *suck up* has two very different meanings, to absorb and to ingratiate; don't confuse them.

Topic Selection Method 2: Read

Sometimes students will comment, when we're conferring about sources for their projects, that doing library research feels like being a detective à la Sherlock Holmes. I quite agree. Both detective stories and police procedurals are helpful models for their emphasis on careful observation, verification of seemingly obvious facts, and inductive logic. Although you probably will never deal with an actual crime scene in your library research, you will often face a set of unknowns and the need to reconstruct (or predict) an environment, an event, or someone else's experience. The major difference is that instead of a dead body, your starting point will be something else that rivets your attention and merits investigation.

But, you may ask, what if nothing rivets my attention, and yet I have to produce an essay, speech, or science project based on research? That ailment afflicts everyone at some point—and, left untreated, will cause your research anxiety to soar to the point of paralysis.

The second method I suggest for getting beyond such an impasse is to read *summaries* of the general area or issue your assignment concerns—for instance, French Impressionism—in an encyclopedia or textbook (but not the textbook assigned for your course because you are already familiar with its approach to the subject). Better yet, read at least two summaries and note their different treatments of the same material.

Feel free to start with Google or Wikipedia, but don't stop there. Instead, see whether your school or public library has electronic access to the *Encyclopædia Britannica* or an appropriate subject encyclopedia. You will not be wasting time by using multiple tools, but will be expanding your understanding of your overall topic—and, in the process, verifying facts as every good detective needs to do. You should be able to figure this out for yourself from the library's home page categories, but if you are uncertain, or would prefer to work with a printed encyclopedia (believe it or not, some of the best, most topic-focused ones exist only as bound volumes), then speak with a reference librarian about what is available and where to find it. Similarly, a librarian can advise you how to identify and locate alternative textbooks that cover the topic of your research assignment from different angles. To use the French Impressionism example, you might be using *Gardner's Art through the Ages* as your textbook for class, but there are excellent treatments of the topic in an encyclopedia called—despite its name—*The Dictionary of Art*, available in print or online at most college libraries, and in other standard textbooks such as Janson's *History of Art: The Western Tradition.*

When I suggest that you note how various accounts of a subject differ, I mean that quite literally: use your mind, then use your keyboard (or pencil) to record intriguing facts or ideas in a computer file or notebook you dedicate to your research project. Here is how to make the most of this tactic. As you take notes from an encyclopedia or textbook, *use quotation marks* to indicate that you are transcribing someone else's words verbatim. Or you can rephrase, outline, or diagram key points—adding a reminder to yourself such as *[my summary]* at the beginning or end of each entry. This practice will avoid future confusion because, if you later use those ideas in your own work, it will be clear that you have recast the passages in your own words. In either case, however, be meticulous about recording all of the following information about each text:

- Author's name
- Title of the specific entry in the encyclopedia or chapter in a textbook
- Title of the encyclopedia or textbook as a whole
- City of publication, publisher's name, year of publication
- Page(s) from which you copied or summarized text

(If you are reading an entry in an online work, such as the *Encyclopædia Britannica*, then print out the interesting sections and record as many of these elements as you can easily determine, right on the printout. Do the same on any pages you choose to photocopy from a printed volume.)

The most important caution of all is that whenever and however you touch the work of another person—whether physically, with a highlighter; virtually, by using the copy-and-paste command on a computer; or intellectually, by making a mental note—be aware that neither the ideas nor their expression are your own.

I have two reasons for endorsing the potentially dangerous practice of copying passages from encyclopedias or textbooks, or of restating the information you find there in

---

On Plagiarism

My advice to jump-start your research by taking notes from reference works and textbooks will upset many high school teachers and college professors. As educators, they want students to avoid the cardinal intellectual sin, plagiarism, a term derived from the Latin word for kidnapping—in this case, using someone else's ideas without acknowledgment. Serious thinkers, researchers, and writers will always give credit where credit is due. Unfortunately, some people, who surely know better, are sloppy or unscrupulous about attributing ideas and phrases to those from whom they have "borrowed" them. Anyone found guilty of stealing the work of others is likely to have his or her career and reputation damaged forever. I call plagiarism the Frumious Bandersnatch of research, after Lewis Carroll's admonition to "shun the Frumious Bandersnatch." (From "Jabberwocky," lines 7–8, in *Through the Looking-Glass, and What Alice Found There.* London: Macmillan and Co., 1872.)

---

your own words. One is that I want you to resist another cardinal sin, procrastination—otherwise known as stalling—when it comes to library research. Transcribing information is a good way to do that because (a) it helps focus your attention on the project; (b) it involves a bit of effort, so you will have an early stake in the result; (c) it gives you some momentum; and (d) not least of all, it yields relevant material to ponder as you proceed. Furthermore, having explained what plagiarism is and warned you that it is wrong, I trust you not to do it.

My other reason for recommending the write-it-down-from-the-get-go approach is that, since the purpose of library research is to discover sources, you might as well adopt the habit of systematically recording both *what* you find and exactly *where* you find it from the start, even long before you settle on a precise topic. What might seem to you like busy work may spark an insight later on that will shape your entire project. A big bonus of keeping a running account of everything you use is that you will not waste time assembling references for the bibliography (often called works cited) of your paper because all the necessary details about your sources will already be in one place: your online file or notebook.

I have more to say about procrastination (how not to let it bog you down), plagiarism (how to respect the boundary between your own work and that of others), and documentation (how to acknowledge the sources you use) in later chapters. I introduce these concerns now, however, because if you go wrong in any of these areas, your research project will be doomed.

Topic Selection Method 3: Browse

Another way to track down a simpatico topic is often right under your nose in the form of sources listed in a textbook or an encyclopedia, or ones mentioned by your instructor in class. Turn to the further readings section of a book or journal article you have recently read in the course, the tone or argument of which attracts you, and then turn to your library's online catalog to determine which of the books listed are available in your local collection. Search either by author (last name first is usually the format) or by title (leaving off *A*, *An*, or *The* if it happens to be the first word), and then look over the hit(s) resulting from your search. (Do not just Google the author or title of a book you think sounds interesting, because those results will be confusing and may not tell you, in any case, whether your library owns the book.)

Assuming your library's catalog includes the book you had in mind, and that its status is given as "on shelf" or the equivalent, then print out or write down its complete call number—think of this as its address—and figure out from a directory, map, or sign exactly where the book should reside in the building. (If you don't see that directional information posted, or don't understand how to navigate to your goal, ask staff at any public service desk.) Then go into the stacks—where books with call numbers like the one you want are shelved—where a bonanza awaits you. On both sides of the book you set out to find will be others on the same, or closely related, themes. Hence you can browse, or scan, your way to an exciting topic of your own by standing in one place. In fact, even if the book you want is checked out, missing, or otherwise unavailable at the time, it is smart to go to the shelf where it would be to see what else there is.

Most library catalogs allow you to search using a call number instead of an author's name, book title, or keywords. The result of such a search is a list of all the books in the collection that should be on the shelf if nothing is checked out, misshelved, or missing. This is virtual browsing and an extremely powerful technique that requires just one relevant call number (which you will have discovered from your initial author or title search) at the start. Ask a reference librarian how to do this if you don't see it as a choice on the catalog screen.

Call Numbers and Classifications

The most common types of call numbers (which are identification symbols unique to each book in a library's collection) come from either the Dewey or the Library of Congress classification scheme. Dewey call numbers consist of three numerals followed by a decimal element. Library of Congress call numbers are more like car license plates, with one or more capital letters, followed by a whole number up to 9999, then a decimal, another capital letter, and yet more numerals. Most libraries use just one of these, but if you ever visit more than one library in the course of your research, you could end up browsing for books on, say, the history of aviation under 629.13...in a Dewey collection and under TL515...in a Library of Congress collection. Each library's online catalog will tell you the precise call number to look for there. This is nothing to worry about, just an idiosyncrasy to be aware of.

Why does this work? Nearly all North American libraries, whether they exist in one room (like a high school's media center) or in vast buildings, arrange volumes on their shelves by subject. Instead of organizing their book collections in other plausible ways—for instance, by date, color, or language—libraries place books with similar content next to each other. As a result, when you arrive in the stack aisle where a specific book is located, you will discover that all its neighbors are also its relatives, intellectually speaking.

If you've never had the pleasure of browsing the shelves in a library, here's the drill once you get to the spot you've targeted. (Hint: Always take your PDA or a notebook and pencil with you when you go off to the stacks. This is essential equipment for any safari.)

1. Carefully examine the book you came to find. This
   means take it off the shelf and notice its year of publication (which will appear on either the title page or the
   other side of it, where copyright information is given).
   Look at the table of contents to see what the various
   chapters are about. Flip through the text to determine if
   there are diagrams, maps, photographs, or other features
   that look interesting. Pay attention to the author's notes
   and documentation—in other words, ask yourself
   whether this book would point you to additional helpful
   sources. Lastly, skim any indexes, looking for names or
   events or concepts that pertain to your tentative topic. If,
   by this point, you think the book could be useful for your
   research project, then take it with you to check out. If it
   doesn't look good for your purpose, either put it back
   exactly where you found it or leave it on a nearby table
   for library staff to reshelve. (Next to mutilating or de-
   facing materials, the worst thing users do in libraries is
   misshelve items. Even though this is seldom intentional,
   it has the net effect of stealing because others will not find
   the book where it belongs, at least until someone happens to notice and correct the problem. When in doubt
   about its proper location, don't put any book back when
   you are done with it.)

2. Now repeat these steps with books on the same shelf or
   adjacent ones. I don't mean that you should handle
   dozens of other volumes, but just a few that somehow
   strike you, from their titles or appearance, as beneficial
   for your current enterprise, namely, choosing an interesting topic you can live with (and enjoy, I hope) for
   several weeks.

3. If you started with more than one call number from the
   online catalog, and especially if your imagination has not

been piqued by the books you've already seen, then go to the other areas of the stacks and continue the browsing process there. It's not unusual for several books that you would say are all about one topic—for instance, native peoples of Australia and New Zealand—to sit in different places in a library's collection. One might have a call number in the anthropology area of the stacks, another in politics, another in the history of the region, and yet another in religion. (Why does this scattering happen? Because catalogers—library specialists whose job it is to describe materials so that users like you and me can discover their existence in online catalogs and their physical presence on a shelf in the collection—do not always agree on what a book is about. Consequently one person may give it a call number for an area of knowledge that is not where another cataloger would assign the same book.) In any case, before you leave the stacks, with or without books to check out and take home, write a few lines in your PDA or notebook about what you found (or expected to, but didn't) and your impressions of how authors have looked at the topic you have in mind. For example, if your browsing in the stacks convinces you that most scholars have treated human cloning as unlikely or unethical, make a note to that effect for yourself, including the call number(s) where you found their books. Remember that you are not yet to the real research stage of the process; you are at the beginning, trying to settle on an interesting general topic. Depending on how your thinking and investigation develop, you may well return to the same shelves before long. Most important, jot down your own new thoughts about how you might approach some aspect of the topic.

Topic Selection Method 4: Look

All college-level history and humanities courses, many social science courses, and some science courses include, in addition to a textbook and critical readings, actual primary sources—that is, evidence created by or near whatever you are studying. A primary source can be, for instance, a sonnet, a speech, a law, a photograph, a musical score, a stock market chart, an equation, a computer graph of a drug interaction, or just about anything else—provided that it can be shared. (If you have a brilliant idea or a harrowing experience, but never tell a soul about it, you leave no clue and no source.)

I discuss primary sources at length later on but bring them up here because one way to discover a captivating topic is to look deeply into a primary source to see what it tells you and to attempt to understand it in its original context. When experts in any field describe how they become hooked on a topic, they often will allude to pondering a primary source.

Topic Selection Method 5: Link

The final technique for divining a topic is somewhat advanced, but I want to suggest it anyway. It is to think about what you already know that relates, however distantly, to the gist of your research assignment and then try to connect the dots in an unusual way. Say your assignment is to write about some aspect of American rural life between 1865 and 1914, and you remember having heard that social dancing was a popular pastime in that era, plus you have an ancestor's diary that describes a sermon claiming a ticket to a dance is a ticket to hell: you could decide to work those threads together and investigate the conflict between religion and entertainment around 1900. Instead of gazing inward at a primary source for a topic idea, you would be gazing outward at several factors that could illuminate one another. Not surprisingly, this approach will become easier as you bring more experience and learning to it.

Have Topic—Now What?

Let's assume you have settled on a topic that interests you and that falls within the scope of your research assignment. Let's also assume that you have run your idea past your instructor, either in person or by e-mail, and that he has approved it. (This is not a necessary part of the research process, unless so specified in the assignment, but it is a prudent one. Knowing from the start that your teacher thinks your topic has merit will remove some of the uncertainty of research and hence reduce your anxiety along the way.) Finally, let's assume that you will *not* be conducting a scientific experiment in a laboratory or other formal setting. I add this last point because my premise is that research topics, like iron ore, need to be refined before you can shape anything useful or beautiful (your own insights and argument) from them. The trouble with experimental research, and the reason I exclude it, is that its steps—hypothesis, sampling, instrumentation, controls, replication, and all the rest—are so specific that the library research involved (to provide the supporting literature review mentioned in chapter 1) has a very different character. Instead of *narrowing* their topic before searching for relevant sources, experimental researchers usually want to *expand* it to see whether the theory they are using has been tested in another field, and if so, how and with what results. That approach deserves its own treatment in a more advanced book by a practicing scientist; ask a science professor to recommend one.

Surprise! I am not going to tell you how to refine your topic and proceed to identify sources—at least not yet. In fact, I'm going to urge you *not* to go near the library or turn on your computer for at least another day. You may think that twenty-four hours from start to finish of a research paper is ample time. If I can persuade you otherwise—not just for the sake of your grade and your education, but because a longer process is in fact easier to manage and a lot less painful than a compressed one—then I will have met one of my goals in writing this book. See the Research Timelines appendix for suggestions.

It's not that you deserve a reward for reaching this point—having "found" a general topic—however you did it. My advice comes from years of watching students nearly drown in a sea of sources because they rush from the shore into the waves, clutching their topic like a surfboard but without any idea of how to ride it or what to do when the tide turns. This happens because students ignore the most important element in the research process: engaging their imagination *before* they sally forth.

Brainstorming

What I recommend you do now is to play with your topic, ideally (a) in a comfortable setting, (b) with a friend or two with no stake in your particular project (although they may be classmates in your same course), and (c) with a computer file or notebook or what I will more often call, from here on, a research log. If you used either Topic Selection Method #2, and have read and taken notes from an encyclopedia or textbook, or #3, and have browsed in the library's stacks, then you have already begun your research log. If you arrived at your general topic via another route, now is the time to create one.

About Research Logs

Since the purpose of a research log is to keep track of all your steps and thoughts as you work through the stages of your investigation, you will want to choose the medium you are most comfortable with. If you always have a digital device with you, then keep your research log on it. Being from the old school, I prefer to use a new notebook of any size or shape—making sure to label it with my name and contact information, in case I lose it—or to appropriate empty pages (at least twenty sheets) in the back of a spiral notebook I am no longer using. I also choose not to keep my research log in the same place as my lecture notes, assignments, or other material from the course in question. Having a dedicated log reminds me that my research project is special, not just another assignment.

Whatever you decide to do, your research log should be both portable and handy. The point of maintaining a research log from start to finish of a project is so that you can quickly capture all your ideas and steps when they are still hot, just as you would in a laboratory notebook as you work on an experiment. Reconstituting what you thought and did after the fact, even just a few hours later, will inevitably lead you to edit your experience and lose momentum.

As to layout of my research log, I use the right-hand pages as a sort of diary (definitely not for publication!), making entries with the date and place where I did something related to my research—whether thinking, brainstorming with friends, conferring with my instructor, searching a database, browsing in the library stacks, or any other activity. I write down a phrase about what I did or read and (if I don't finish something) where I left off, all just practical notes to keep myself on target and to prevent accidentally repeating the same step several days later—and wasting precious time—because I've lost my train of thought. I use the left-hand page opposite to jot stray ideas, alternative points of view, the title and author of any interesting book I turn up, call numbers if I've used my library's online catalog, new questions I might want to consider or discuss with an expert, sometimes even expletives or doodles. You get the picture: it's my mental scrapbook for that research project. Obviously, you can do the same things with a PDA or in a computer file.

Where, you may wonder, do I keep my actual research notes as I read and evaluate the sources I discover? That depends. For a short research project—say, one where I will ultimately rely on just a handful of sources—I will include my summary notes and any exact quotations, including page numbers, in my research log itself, using a separate page for each source and being careful to record accurately its complete bibliographic (descriptive) information, so that I won't need to scramble later as I compile my works cited list. For a longer, more extensive research project, I prefer either an ancient method (large index cards I can annotate and rearrange) or a modern one (a computer file) for keeping notes on whatever I turn up. In either case, I also make brief chronological entries of my research activities in my log throughout the process.

One big advantage of maintaining a research log, besides keeping yourself focused, is that you can easily recap both what you've done and how it went when you confer with your teacher, a librarian, or anyone else about your project. A second, but longer term, advantage is that each research project you undertake will build on the process you've used previously. So save your research logs!

Bibliographic Software:
Good Idea, but with a Caveat

Related in purpose to a research log is a citation management program to help with the recordkeeping (or source documentation) part of the library research process. The two most widely used in higher education are EndNote and RefWorks, which may be available free or at a nominal cost to students and faculty. Ask a reference librarian about their availability on your campus and whether there are brief training sessions you can attend. Both EndNote and Ref-Works are marvelously helpful tools for advanced research, but, like any new software, they take time to master and continual use to maintain your expertise.

Either program allows you to connect directly to almost any library's catalog and import records (descriptions of the books and other sources in the collection) relevant to your research into a file you create for that purpose. In addition, both EndNote and RefWorks have ways to import references to journal articles from any database you are ever likely to search, often with a single mouse click. They also let you type in citations by hand, something you'll appreciate if you've conducted an interview, for example, or discovered

(continued on next page)

---

just a few letters you want to use within a large manuscript collection. Once you have source citations in your EndNote or RefWorks file, you can add your own notes about each item, including precise quotes you may want to use. You can also sort citations (by call number, for instance, so you won't waste time getting to all the right shelves in the stacks), and insert the ones you actually want to use for your project directly into your Word document. In short, these programs will help you manage your (research) baggage.

Best of all, bibliographic managers will instantly do your grunt work formatting footnotes and endnotes, plus the list of works cited that goes at the end of your paper, into whichever bibliographic style your assignment specifies—complete with proper indentions, punctuation, fonts, and all the other fussy business involved.

Having just described their immense benefits and abundant features, I will tell you honestly, as someone who tutors students in both EndNote and RefWorks, that I would not recommend you tackle one *until* you begin a research project that is lengthy (several weeks) in duration and will involve at least several dozen sources you will need to weave into your own argument. Only then will your investment of time and persistence really pay off. Nearly all college juniors and seniors (and definitely all graduate students) should master one of these programs, but few freshmen and sophomores are likely to feel the return outweighs the effort.

Back to Brainstorming

Let's suppose you have some familiarity with the topic you plan to explore—for example, Manhattan as a setting in two

---

About Argument

The word *argument* in the context of most writing and all research projects just means an explanation of the ideas that the writer or researcher derives from his or her work. A successful argument must be clear to its intended audience, substantiated by sources, and not obvious. There is a widespread, but wrong, belief among students that a successful argument must also be "new." The actual case is this: a successful argument reveals an idea that is new to you, the researcher, in a way (and with a voice) that is new to your audience. Ideally, a successful argument will also persuade your audience of its truth, but I wouldn't count on that. Internal consistency and clarity of reasoning, balancing your sources with your insights, is a more realistic goal in college.

---

novels, F. Scott Fitzgerald's *The Great Gatsby* (published in 1925) and J. D. Salinger's *The Catcher in the Rye* (published in 1951). In other words, you've read both works recently—and have copies of them in hand—and can draw on personal impressions of New York City from several visits there. Let's also suppose that your assignment is to write an eight- to ten-page essay, using at least three scholarly sources, in which you will not only enumerate similarities and differences between the two novels but also develop your own insights into a well-reasoned argument. And let's finally pretend that you have two weeks before the paper is due and that you are going to get started on it today.

Brainstorming in this situation, after you have read the two novels and developed an interesting notion about them—New York City as a location in both plots—should be fast and fun. I estimate it will take you an hour, maybe less, to engage your mental gears and start your creative engine in preparation for your research trip.

Earlier I said that brainstorming is a way to play with your topic, but let me be more specific. **Brainstorming means examining your topic from a variety of angles—keeping an open mind and an open research log, the former to invite new ideas and the latter to house them.** As I mentioned, it is most productive if you brainstorm with a friend or two in a congenial place, for instance, while having a meal or study break together. But if that is not possible, or not your style of working, then you can brainstorm by yourself anywhere that you won't be distracted. The point is, don't delay, because if you skip this stage of the library research process, you will almost certainly waste time and energy later on.

And I would add another caution: don't dismiss brainstorming because you fear that someone may steal your topic, or that brainstorming is somehow unethical because you are soliciting ideas from others. Both worries are false: brainstorming is a perfect opportunity to test your premises and to think outside the box of your own head. Treat the people you brainstorm with as readers or hearers of your final presentation, in other words, as part of your future audience (whether they will be or not).

Guide to Brainstorming

Here is a list of issues to brainstorm about. Don't let the number of steps or their wording dismay you. I explain them as I go. The good news is that it does not take very long to think through them all, and you will get faster with practice as you encounter a wide variety of research projects.

1. **State your assignment in one sentence and your general research topic in another.**

Write these two sentences in your research log, then read them out loud to your brainstorming buddies so they understand the scope of what you're proposing to do. (If they are not clear about your project, it's an early sign of big trouble, so it would be best to halt the proceedings—sort of like a rain delay at a baseball game—until you can go back to your class notes or instructor for guidance. Another solution is to devote a couple of hours to Topic Selection Method #2, reading more background on your topic in order to sharpen your thoughts, and hence your statement of what you want to investigate.)

2. **Have a free-for-all discussion about your topic, with the aim of generating several specific research questions to explore.**

Three or four questions are adequate for most undergraduate research projects, but if you and your friends are on a roll and think of more than that, keep going. Write down everything you come up with in your research log, being careful to phrase each idea as an actual question, ending with a question mark. The most fruitful research questions, by the way, begin with the interrogatives *why* or *how*. The other four questions journalists always ask—*who, what, where,* and *when*—are also essential for library research, but they seldom lead to an interesting argument (unless the facts surrounding a topic are a genuine mystery, like the identity of Jack the Ripper). *Why* questions and *how* questions offer much more room for your own insights. Above all, do not veto or censor any question that occurs to you because you think it would be impossible, too difficult, or too time consuming to answer.

◣ MARY'S MAXIM #4: Never Reject a Crazy Idea, Just Record It

3. **For each specific question, imagine what kinds of information (both facts and opinions) would help you answer it *and* where that kind of information would logically come from.**

Use bullet points under each question in your research log to keep track of these thoughts. For instance, if one question you have written down is, "How accurately did F[itzgerald] and S[alinger] depict social class in their respective novels?" you might list beneath it:

- Population and income figures for New York City in the mid-1920s and early 1950s—statistics collected by national, state, or municipal government agencies [factual information]
- Accounts of social life—from contemporary local newspapers [could be a mix of factual information and opinion or observation]
- Early reviews of each novel—did reviewers comment on the character portrayals?—reviews—probably in newspapers and popular periodicals in 1925–26 and 1951–52 [contemporary opinion]

Then move on quickly to your next research question. Remember, you are toying with possibilities, not committing yourself to a specific research path or argument at this stage. For an average-length research paper such as this you will not be pursuing all of your questions or all of the kinds of information you come up with while brainstorming. The goal is to speculate and capture ideas. (*Speculate* derives from a Latin word meaning *to spy out* or *to examine,* exactly the mindset you want. An alternative, also Latinate, word I like is *to prospect,* meaning to explore an area, in the sense of a miner looking for gold.)

The next two considerations are, in my view, the most important for any library research project, because your thoughts—bolstered by those of your brainstorming compatriots—will shape your subsequent plan of action more than anything else.

4. **What physical formats would you expect your sources of information to come in?**

On the surface, this sounds like a no-brainer, but it's not. When students first ponder this question, many name two, and only two, things: books (long) and articles (short). These are the only formats they think a library can provide, doubtless because that's all they have encountered so far. Given a choice, they would prefer to conduct all their research using articles they can get electronically at home, but they suspect they may have to visit a library building to check out several printed books.

If this describes your experience, then now is the time to expand your horizon. Here is an incomplete roster, with minimal elaboration, of the kinds of materials that exist in almost any public or college library, and in many high school libraries as well. You will find definitions of unfamiliar terms in this book's glossary, or in any dictionary.

- Printed books by one or more authors
- Printed books containing chapters by different writers, usually with a named editor
- Printed reference works, often in multivolume sets, that convey factual information, and sometimes interpretation as well

- Printed anthologies, collections of writings (such as short stories) that were originally published elsewhere
- Printed articles in magazines, popular periodicals, or scholarly journals
- Printed articles in newspapers
- Printed documents or official publications from a government, organization, association, or business
- Printed photographs or illustrations, including art reproductions
- Printed maps or charts
- Printed music scores
- Printed statistical tables
- "Raw" numbers, coded but not yet analyzed, in electronic form called data sets
- "Cooked" numbers, published after data has been analyzed
- Three-dimensional objects, such as globes or models
- Audio and video recordings
- Handwritten, typewritten, or printed transcripts of interviews or speeches
- Handwritten or typewritten manuscripts
- Archives, collections of documents from a person, family, or organization
- Any of the above in microformat
- Any of the above in digital format, whether as part of a searchable database of similar information sources or existing as an independent entity

What all of these physical formats have in common is that they are *recorded* and hence can be *shared*. **An experience, idea, or insight that never leaves the mind of the thinker is not, and never can be, a source.**

Look again at the research questions you have written in your log and the notes you have under them about what sort of information would help you answer them and where that information might come from. Now look at the list above and assign plausible physical formats to each research question. To return to the example from step 3 of the brainstorming process, but now adding physical format(s) under each of your ideas:

How accurately did F[itzgerald] and S[alinger] depict social class in their respective novels?

- Population and income figures for New York City in the mid-1920s and early 1950s—statistics collected by national, state, or municipal government agencies [factual information]
    - Printed federal census volumes for New York from 1920 and 1950
- Accounts of social life—from contemporary local newspapers [could be a mix of factual information and opinion or observation]
    - New York City newspapers from the two periods, in digital or microfilm format
    - Printed books of memoirs by prominent people who observed New York social life during these times
- Early reviews of each novel—did reviewers comment on the character portrayals? —reviews—probably in newspapers and popular periodicals in 1925–26 and 1951–52 [contemporary opinion]
    - Newspapers and periodicals from the year each novel was published (and the following year, to play it safe); may be in printed and bound format on the library shelves, or in microformat, or digitized

Why, you may wonder, does the physical format of information sources matter, except as a convenience to the researcher? It matters extremely because every information source is a package having its own physical characteristics: shape, dimensions, weight, sturdiness or fragility, commonness (many copies exist) or uniqueness (the library owns the only copy in existence, as with a manuscript), and need for auxiliary equipment or expert assistance. Not surprisingly, each general kind of source will live in a different place in a library, just as a business will stock inventory by size in its warehouse. Books live on shelves, archives and manuscript collections live in secure vaults, microformats live in special file cabinets, digital images and data sets live on servers somewhere. You get the idea.

Furthermore, libraries list what they have in different ways, often based solely on the physical features of material. Book-shaped sources may be identified via an online catalog; archival and manuscript collections kept in folders and cartons may be described in a database; microformat sources or periodical subscriptions may be listed on a poster affixed to a wall. All too often, the only clue about where something is will be a staff member's memory, as in "Only Ms. Young knows where that is. We'll call her and find out for you."

I know that Google and other search engines seem, and sometimes claim, to include everything of interest, but they don't, and won't anytime soon. So forget about Googling as a one-stop solution; it's just one useful tactic among many. In any case, identifying the existence of a particular, likely information source—even learning that it is held by your specific library—is not sufficient for your research purposes. You still need to know *exactly* where to go, and what to do, to locate the item on the premises. If you spend a minute or two at the start of your research imagining the probable physical formats—think of them as containers—of information that may be useful, then you will not overlook anything. At some point in your research, you can go back to your brainstorming notes in your research log and ask your instructor or a reference librarian whether the physical formats you imagined will indeed be both helpful and available.

5. **What is the nature of those sources—primary, secondary, or some of each?**

Understanding the concept of source, both in general and as it relates to a specific investigation, is the biggest challenge you will face in any research project. As with the physical format consideration I just described, it is important to speculate as you brainstorm about the *primary* versus *secondary* status of the sources you will want—all the more so if your assignment specifies that you should base your research on one or the other, or both, of these source types.

No one grasps the distinction between primary and secondary source the first time they encounter it, so you are not alone. What most students will recite, if asked, is a definition they have memorized that goes like this: "A primary source is something written at the time [of the event I am studying], and a secondary source is a later comment about it by someone else." This is not wrong; it is just simplistic and of little help in real-life research. It is like saying, "Lightning comes before thunder," without elaboration, or like quoting the Pythagorean theorem and then not being able to apply it.

A much better way to grasp the distinction is to substitute the phrase *first-hand evidence* for *primary source* and the word *interpretation* for *secondary source*. You must, however, be aware that these are not mutually exclusive categories—which is precisely why the concept of source is so hard. To use the September 11, 2001, terror attacks as an example: primary sources include both inanimate evidence (sounds, vibrations,

smoke, debris) and human evidence from those who partic-
ipated in some way (victims who called for help, survivors,
eyewitnesses, rescuers, journalists). Secondary sources, in
contrast, come exclusively from people, because only the
human mind can interpret. For 9/11, secondary sources
sprang up within minutes following the attacks and will
continue to be created in the future, probably forever, and
recorded in every physical format imaginable.

This distinction between primary source and secondary
source seems obvious until you look closely. Let's consider
an actual source from the aftermath of the terror attacks, a
guest editorial by U.S. Representative Charles B. Rangel,
who represents northern Manhattan in Congress.* In it he
describes his personal reaction to the events of 9/11, his
caution against blaming Arab or Islamic people as a group,
and his support for legislation to fund military retaliation
and to support victims' families. Does this article count as a
primary source, a secondary source, both, neither, or what?
The answer is, *it depends on your research question.* If you
are asking how New York City's black leaders responded
to the terror attacks, then Mr. Rangel's editorial could be one
of your primary sources. His words, appearing in a major
newspaper nine days after the event, come as close as possible
to capturing his thoughts and actions at the time. If instead
you are asking how the United States government should
have responded to the terror attacks, then Mr. Rangel's
editorial is a secondary source because he is expressing
only his own opinion (commentary, interpretation), which
you are using—probably with the opinions of several other
officials—to bolster your argument.

*Charles Rangel, "An open letter on the terrorist attack against the United States,"
New York Amsterdam News, September 20, 2001, 12.

It is not unusual for one physical source to have two roles, just like a trick image that seems to project or recede from its background depending on the viewer's angle. The distinction between primary and secondary sources is subtle, yet one every researcher must consider early in any project, so I suggest making this part of your brainstorming routine. As you gain more experience with library research, and as you encounter projects in a variety of fields, deciding whether a given source is primary or secondary will become easier.

➤ MARY'S MAXIM #5: Practice Thinking About Sources

Some students like to imagine that they are investigative journalists seeking informants to "make" their story. If this scenario appeals to you, just remember that interviewing is only one of many methods of research. Good journalists also rely on published accounts and other sources of evidence for background and opposing views.

Ultimately, teachers are the best sources about sources. In every class you take, whether or not it has a research assignment (but especially if it does), ask your instructor and any guest speakers to comment about how experts in that area go about their business of discovery: what types of questions they ask, what methods they use in their investigations, what primary and secondary sources they need, how they communicate new knowledge to other experts and to the general public, and related aspects of inquiry. Your textbook may address some of these topics, but there is nothing like hearing a specialist's views to help you grasp the complexity of research.

6. **What points of view are likely to be present in your sources of information, either primary or secondary?**

This is a brainstorming question that usually takes about five minutes to address. Next to each type of source you've listed in your research log, add a note (I use a different color font or pen to do this) about what you imagine may have been the perspective—even the ulterior motive—of the source's creator at the time. For instance, let's suppose your research question is, "How did Americans' views of women physicians change in the second half of the twentieth century?" You've decided you want to identify statements from leaders of both medical and religious organizations, plus articles in news and women's magazines, on that subject. Think ahead about where sources may be coming from so that you will more easily be able to read between the lines once you have them in front of you. You might jot down phrases such as *traditional homemaker, fear of competition, asserting feminist rights,* or *will result in salary equalization.* Although you don't want to preempt your own opinions about your eventual sources, it is smart to begin your research with a dash of caution about them. Don't agonize about this; just make a few notes in your log and move on.

A good way to sensitize yourself to what is called political rhetoric (even about topics that have nothing to do with politics in the strict sense) is to spend an hour every week reading essays about a current event in periodicals or newspapers of different editorial persuasions—for instance, *The Nation* (relatively liberal), *The New Republic* (relatively centrist), and *National Review* (relatively conservative). You could do the same thing by reading select blogs or watching commentary programs on a variety of TV channels. The point is to compare the ways writers with different convictions phrase their ideas, so that you will recognize where on the spectrum your sources come from. Not incidentally, exposure to well-crafted essays, regardless of their bias, will help you sharpen and articulate your own argument later on. Also not incidentally, you will learn where to go for opposing viewpoints when you want some to contrast with your own.

7. Who cares?

This is the final brainstorming issue, and like the previous one on anticipating bias, it can be quickly dispatched. I grant that "Who cares?" sounds like a snippy question, but all it means is that you should make a list in your research log of the key players who have probably had something to say about your general topic. Key players are usually not specific people—although they might be—but rather whole disciplines, organizations, and interest groups whose members have weighed in on the research questions you plan to address.

Here are some of the research questions I used earlier in this discussion of brainstorming, now with the addition of this final angle.

Why should *you* care who cares? For the same reason that you should predict the physical formats of relevant sources: because the information and opinions you may want often hide in different places, depending on who created or expressed or recorded or published them. Just as you will not find a music recording in the same place as a city map, you will not find scholarly work by lawyers and chemists in the same place. Different voices, different rooms—to paraphrase the title of one of Truman Capote's books—and yet you may want to hear both in your research.

The Internet may be a great unifier, search engines may claim to retrieve everything relevant on a topic, some databases cross disciplinary lines, general newspapers offer a vast

Research Question	Who Cares
How accurately did F[itzgerald] and S[alinger] depict social class in their respective novels (*The Great Gatsby* and *The Catcher in the Rye*)?	• Literary critics • Social historians • Economists
How should the United States government have responded to the 9/11 terror attacks?	• Politicians • Political commentators • Survivors • Military leaders • Heads of foreign governments • Islamic groups and media in the U.S.
How did Americans' views of women physicians change in the second half of the twentieth century?	• American Medical Association • Women's rights organizations • Medical school deans • Sociologists

array of facts and views, printed and digitized collections of important sources (both primary and secondary) exist for broad subject areas—but at some point in your research you will need a specialized source intended for a specialized audience. Think ahead, as you wind down your brainstorming, about who might care enough to generate such sources.

Lastly—common courtesy, so I won't give this point its own number—if you brainstormed with the help of friends, thank them and ask if they'd like to read your final paper or attend your presentation. And if they made a significant contribution to your work, remember to acknowledge them in a note in your final paper or by a sentence in your oral presentation.

Recap of Brainstorming Issues

1. State your assignment in one sentence and your general research topic in another.
2. Have a free-for-all discussion about your topic, with the aim of generating several specific research questions to explore.
3. For each specific question, imagine what kinds of information (both facts and opinions) would help you answer it and where that kind of information would logically come from.
4. What physical formats would you expect your sources of information to come in?
5. What is the nature of those sources—primary, secondary, or some of each?
6. What points of view are likely to be present in your sources of information, either primary or secondary?
7. Who cares?

Where We Go from Here

If you think about your library research project as a party you will host several weeks from now, then brainstorming is like planning the menu and estimating how much food you will need to prepare. The next step is to choose recipes and make sure you have all the ingredients and utensils, or know where you can get them. Those are the two topics of the next chapter, only instead of multiple recipes, I suggest one master research strategy, and instead of ingredients and utensils, I describe reference tools of many useful sorts. When you see how the tools fit into the strategy, you'll realize the wisdom of brainstorming first.

3

Strategy and Tools for Discovery

As you've gathered by now, successful library research involves a mix of concepts, procedures, and guesswork. You can't simply plug numbers into a formula and trust the answer will come out right. When you conduct library research, you are engaging your mind at every stage as you imagine what sources of information and opinion ought to exist, predict how to zero in on them, assess their actual usefulness for answering your research questions, and sleuth for alternative sources if the first ones don't work.

After you've brainstormed, look over the research questions you've written in your log, then prioritize them by how interesting they now seem to you. You may well decide, especially for a short project, to concentrate on just one of your research questions, but it's wise to have others handy. The most common complaint I hear from students when they are midway through the library research process is, "I need to change my topic." Although there may be a valid reason for this—for example, if all available sources are in a foreign language the student doesn't read—usually the crisis arises from deadline panic or two predicaments that I call too-much-ness and not-enough-ness. Too-much-ness occurs when you discover dozens (perhaps thousands) of sources that relate to your topic. Not-enough-ness is the opposite problem, when your initial effort turns up few (or no) sources.

Deadline panic may have no remedy in a given situation, but too-much-ness and not-enough-ness almost always do if you take time to rethink and recast your search. When the

urge to quit comes over you—and it will during some research projects—my advice is not to abandon your topic,
but to turn instead to your trusty research log and decide to
concentrate on another of your original research questions.
That way you can build on all your preliminary thinking and
background work because you will not be starting from
scratch. Plus, you won't need to enlist your friends for another round of brainstorming.

  MARY'S MAXIM #6: THOSE WHO
BAIL MAY WELL FAIL

The essence of the library research process is the progression from topic selection, to the research questions you
articulate when you brainstorm, to a search strategy appropriate for your project involving tools of various sorts, to
answers (your sources) others have had to similar research
questions, and finally to your own insight from which you
can craft your argument. Let's look again at the flowchart
I suggested earlier, to review where we are now. The two
shaded segments are the theme of this chapter. Keep in mind
that the priceless ingredient of your own imagination suf-
fuses the entire process and prepares the way for insight.

Defining Search Strategy and Tactics

The purpose of a search strategy is to help you answer your
research questions thoroughly, efficiently, and—this is key—
appropriately for your assignment. Whenever I use the phrase
search strategy, singular or plural, I mean the overall plan for a
library research project, the means by which one discovers

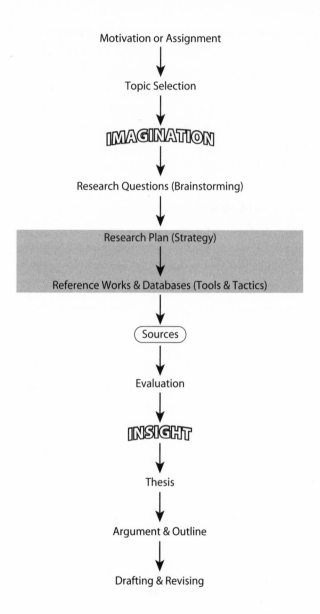

Figure 3.1: Diagram of the Library Research Process

sources (background information, facts, opinion) related to a research question. *Tactics* are the actions and decisions necessary to implement that plan. A well-devised and well-executed search strategy will save you time because each stage leads to the next in an orderly fashion. Provided you think critically throughout the process, a search strategy will propel you forward to the moment of insight I've mentioned, the instant (which can come at any point) when you see how your own ideas can work with facts and opinions from your sources to make an interesting argument.

Although I often use the word *recipe* when I recommend a search strategy to a student, I don't mean that literally. Unlike a cookbook recipe, both the ingredients (reference tools and databases) in a search strategy and the ways of combining them (research tactics) will vary, sometimes greatly, from project to project. To succeed as a researcher you need to understand the master plan and the choices you can make at each point. Then, with a little experience, you'll be able to modify your strategy easily for all your subsequent research efforts.

There are several standard search strategies, but in this book I concentrate on just one of them, the one that works best for most college research projects. After I present it in entirety, I discuss each of its components separately and suggest options to try if any step in the strategy doesn't work for you—that is, doesn't yield the sources you expect.

Basic Search Strategy

1. Read background information on your research questions in one or more specialized, as opposed to general, encyclopedias.

2. Begin to compile several lists (in your research log) and
continue this practice throughout the library research
process. The most important lists include
   a. Relevant terms or phrases for your research, plus
   synonyms for them;
   b. Call numbers you encounter for relevant books;
   c. Subject headings you encounter for relevant books
   and descriptive phrases you encounter in databases;
   d. Names of experts who have studied your topic or
   written about your research questions, and organizations concerned with them;
   e. Titles of scholarly journals and topic-focused periodicals that publish in the field(s) you are exploring.
3. Search your own library's online catalog for
   a. Specific book sources listed at the end of the encyclopedia articles you have read;
   b. Additional book sources your library owns, using the
   subject heading links used for the specific sources;
   c. Still more book sources your library owns, using
   combinations of keywords.
4. Begin systematic browsing of your library's shelves,
looking on the shelves for all the call numbers you have
established in step 3.
5. Search relevant indexes and databases to identify specific
articles on your topic in both scholarly and popular
publications, including newspapers.
6. Skim everything you locate to determine which sources
may be the most useful and to get leads to additional
specific sources.
7. Return to your library's online catalog to find call
numbers for the additional books you have identified via
footnotes and bibliography entries and to determine if
your library subscribes to the periodicals or newspapers

for which you now have article references. Track these
sources down.

8. Repeat steps 3 through 7 as necessary until you have in
   hand the variety of sources you imagined when you were
   brainstorming, conferring at least once with your instructor during the process.

Eight steps is not bad for such a powerful scheme. The rest
of this chapter elaborates on these eight steps and suggests a
few additions and modifications for highly complex research
projects.

About Keywords

Words or phrases that describe your topic generally, and your
research questions in particular, are called *keywords* or *key
phrases* and these are the terms I use. Keywords are the vocabulary that will lead you to discover and unlock relevant
sources for your project. You can never have too many keywords at the start of your research, but as you proceed, certain ones will prove to be more fruitful than others. Just keep
track of them all in your research log, so they will be handy.

Types of Reference Tools

In the core definitions section of chapter 2, I define the word
tool as anything that either encapsulates common knowledge
or points you to a source. I then allude to three categories
I call fact tools, finding tools, and hybrid tools. Now is the
time to explain what I mean by those terms and to list the
varieties of each type. Note that a tool's format (electronic,

print, or human) does not determine its category; what does is its contribution to the overall search strategy.

Even though I have used the adjective *reference* numerous times already in phrases such as *reference work* or *reference librarian,* I want to be clear about its meaning before we consider its manifestations. **A "reference" anything is a helpful assortment of information that has been gathered, summarized, arranged, and published by human beings and that has some meaningful scope.** People turn to reference tools for quick information fixes, choosing a specific one, such as a dictionary, for a specific need, such as a definition or advice on usage, and trusting that they can easily find what they're after because the tool is organized in a standard way— such as alphabetically, if it is in book format—or has a familiar search interface, if it is electronic. People normally will not read a reference work through from beginning to end, but will just grab and go, treating it as a convenience store of information. To me the prototypical reference work—alas, fast disappearing in the Internet age—is the lowly telephone book, containing both white and yellow pages, the former arranged alphabetically by surname and the latter arranged alphabetically by subject, perhaps with extra sections for government offices, local maps and street locations, seating diagrams for nearby stadiums, zip codes, or emergency evacuation procedures. Although you will probably never need a phone book for a college research project, it is a good model for how different types of factual information can be organized in print format.

FACT TOOLS

Fact tools provide just about any nugget of information you could ever want to know. They are the most familiar kind of reference works because we are surrounded by them—whether we know it or not—from infancy. They package words; numbers; formulas; dates; places; quotations; summaries; laws and regulations; how-to, who-is (or who-was), what-are, and where-to entries of all sorts. The possibilities are infinite; if someone might want to know it, chances are someone else has already compiled it. The trick, of course, is to determine where. What distinguishes a fact tool from a trash heap is that everything in a fact tool meets certain criteria, and that within a given fact tool you, the user, should be able to readily spot and extract the item you want.

If you think of a research project as a car trip you have never made before, then fact tools are the signs along the way that tell where you are and what's ahead, with occasional cautions and announcements of coming attractions. Together with a good road map (your search strategy), they will keep you from wandering off track.

On the following page is a list of the most common varieties of fact tools, grouped by the nature of their content, with a brief phrase to indicate what each does, and a few examples, all of which are printed volumes and some of which are also available in digital format. My guess is that you have already encountered several of them.

I know this chart looks daunting, but the good news is that although there are more fact tools than other kinds (finding and hybrid, which I describe next), they are simpler to grasp and you will seldom need them all for the same project.

Type of Fact Tool	Description	Examples
Almanac (sometimes called a yearbook or miscellany)	Miscellaneous assortment of practical information on a variety of topics	• *Old Farmer's Almanack* • *World Almanac and Book of Facts*
Atlas	Group of maps	• *Atlas of the Civil War* • *One Planet, Many People: Atlas of Our Changing Environment*
Gazetteer	List of places with their location and significance; can be freestanding or part of an atlas	• *Columbia Gazetteer of the World* • *A Literary Gazetteer of England*
Handbook (also called a companion, guide, or manual)	Work, usually a single volume or the electronic equivalent, that brings together a whole array of basic information about a field or topic; its purpose is to save researchers time because it sits on their desks as they read and reflect and write; sometimes it will also provide overview articles, with a list of major sources, and hence will function as a specialized encyclopedia	• *CRC Handbook of Chemistry and Physics* • *Oxford Companion to Ships and the Sea* • *The Friendly Guide to Beethoven* • *Diagnostic and Statistical Manual of Mental Disorders*
Biographical compendium (also referred to as a biographical dictionary, directory, or encyclopedia)	Work that provides relatively short accounts of the lives of prominent people, sometimes limited by nationality, occupation, or whether those included are alive or not	• *Who's Who in America* • *New Dictionary of Scientific Biography* • *Oxford Dictionary of National Biography*
Chronology	Work that organizes events by when they occurred, allowing the user to see concurrences and overlapping durations; most common for human history, geology, and astronomy	• *African American Chronology* • *Calendar of Creative Man* • *Timelines of the 20th Century*
Dictionary (sometimes labeled a glossary or lexicon, especially if it concerns the language of a specialized group or vocabulary related to a specialized activity)	Wordbook intended to help people learn, understand, or correctly use language; the subvarieties are too numerous to list; usually in alphabetical order, but may be arranged by theme	• *The American Heritage Dictionary of the English Language* • *The Oxford-Duden Pictorial Spanish-English Dictionary* • *Dictionary of Contemporary Slang*

Type of Fact Tool	Description	Examples
Thesaurus	Synonym dictionary, the most important type of wordbook for library research because it provides related keywords useful for database searching; arranged by concept or alphabetically	• *Roget's Thesaurus* • *The Synonym Finder*
Concordance	List of words (other than articles and prepositions) in a specific work or group of works by the same person, giving the surrounding text; necessary for studying an author's form of expression	• *Concordance to Bronte's "Wuthering Heights"* • *The Complete Concordance to the Bible, New King James Version*
Quotation book	Selection of memorable sayings, with attribution; may be arranged by person, date, topic, or keywords; extremely helpful for verifying famous phrases	• [Bartlett's] *Familiar Quotations* • *Oxford Dictionary of Humorous Quotations* • *The New Quotable Einstein*
Plot overview	Summaries of the action and characters in select novels, plays, and narrative poems; similar to CliffsNotes® study guides; can be useful toward the beginning of a search strategy	• *Masterplots* • *Masterpieces of Latino Literature*
Directory	Overarching term for any work that identifies people, organizations, government agencies, libraries, archives, and other entities a researcher may wish to contact	• *Directory of Board Certified Medical Specialists* • *Halls of Fame: An International Directory* • *Europa World of Learning*
Statistical abstract	Compilation of data describing a population or economic activity, usually presented in table format with documentation indicating who collected the information and when	• *Historical Statistics of the United States: Earliest Times to the Present* • *OECD Factbook: Economic, Environmental and Social Statistics*

(continued)

Type of Fact Tool	Description	Examples
Style manual	Work that describes a consistent, standard format for documenting sources: the information to include, how to capitalize, indent, italicize references in both notes and bibliographies; each academic field has its own preference on which style students should follow, but you may need to ask your instructor to specify it	• *The Chicago Manual of Style* • *Publication Manual of the American Psychological Association* • *MLA Handbook for Writers of Research Papers*

FINDING TOOLS

Finding tools are the vitamins and minerals of healthy research: neither you nor your project will thrive without them. Or, to revert to the road trip metaphor I used earlier, finding tools are the fuel that moves you forward toward the actual sources that will help you answer your research questions.

I define finding tools as reference works that identify sources in some meaningful fashion. If a finding tool is in print format, it must be organized so that the researcher can home in on sources of probable interest. If it is in electronic format (a database), a finding tool must permit the researcher to explore (search) it in various ways, again with the goal of discovering relevant sources.

In a dream world where all the sources pertaining to your research questions could be lined up on one shelf, or retrieved in entirety from a single database, you would not need finding tools. You could simply poke around the shelf or scroll around the screen and, voilà, the scary part of the research process would be over. No more worrying about

Books All Students Should Have
at Their Fingertips (either bookmark
the digital version or acquire the print one)

1. A collegiate dictionary
2. A thesaurus
3. A hefty college composition textbook with sections on grammar, punctuation, word usage, different types of college writing, standard systems for documenting sources, and the like. After you take the course, keep the textbook as a reference tool. (See the bibliography for a list of some of the commonly used ones.)
4. *After* you have chosen a major, the current edition of the style manual professors in the field expect you to follow when you document your sources. (See the bibliography for full citations.)

Ask family and friends to give you these, or a gift certificate from a bookstore, as presents. Also, check your library's electronic offerings and add links to such important tools to your favorites list. Two other works I suggest are

5. A quotation book that includes entries from living or recent writers and speakers
6. *The Elements of Style* by William Strunk and E. B. White (yes, he is the author of *Charlotte's Web* and *Stuart Little*). Any edition is fine. This small book is important for every writer to read from cover to cover, then refer to often. Its succinct rules for clarity will never be surpassed.

whether you will find enough stuff to do the job, or panicking when you realize there's too much stuff (that is, too many sources) and hence too many potential answers to your research questions.

But since this is only a fantasy, you will need to understand and make wise use of finding tools. Unlike fact tools, which are almost endless in their variety, there are just three types of finding tools—catalogs, indexes, and bibliographies.

A *catalog* is a finding tool that identifies the whole-book sources in a specific collection (and often all of a library's newspaper and periodical subscriptions as well). An *index* is a finding tool that identifies the topics treated in a book (the familiar subject index in the back of a nonfiction volume) or the individual articles appearing in issues of a specific group of periodicals. A *bibliography* is a finding tool that identifies sources of any sort that have a specific scope.

Note in all three definitions my use of the verb *identifies* and the adjective *specific*. **Finding tools are pointers to what exists:** in a given place, within a given universe of similar materials, or on a given subject. I call them finding tools because they help researchers find (determine) sources that may provide partial answers—information and opinions—to their research questions.

In some cases, typically an online catalog or electronic index with links to full texts, a finding tool will literally connect you with a complete source. In other cases, such as a printed index or bibliography, a finding tool will give you a short description of each source, sometimes with the bonus of a summary, called an abstract, an extraordinarily helpful feature for researchers because it allows them to judge the probable relevance of a source before they read it in entirety.

Put another way, a catalog will lead you to what I call macro sources, an index will lead you to what I call micro sources, and a bibliography will lead you to both (and often to other goodies as well, such as unpublished manuscripts or interviews or photographs). If your library were a fine restaurant, then its catalog would be the menu, the indexes it provides would be the chef's repertory arranged by ingredient, and its bibliography would be the server's suggestions about what appetizers, entrées, wines, and desserts go well together—the advice of an expert.

HYBRID TOOLS

Hybrid tools combine the nature and function of both fact and finding tools. To return for the last time to my road trip analogy, think of a hybrid tool as the ignition key that starts your research engine; without it you will go nowhere. Since hybrid tools do two jobs at once, providing facts and pointing to related sources, you could also view them as the utility outfielders, who are also star hitters, of the research game.

So exactly what are hybrid tools? They are first and foremost encyclopedias, whether general (like the *Encyclopædia Britannica*—which is American, despite its name—or its equivalents from other countries or in other languages), focused on a family of disciplines or a certain field (like the *McGraw-Hill Encyclopedia of Science & Technology* or the *Encyclopedia of Religion*), or specialized on a single broad topic (like *The Holocaust Encyclopedia*). Interestingly, quite a few encyclopedias do not use that word in their titles, but instead call themselves the *Dictionary of [Whatever]*. Do not let tool names fool you; it's their role in the research process that matters. Also, as I noted earlier on the chart of fact tools, some handbooks function as encyclopedias.

Entries in encyclopedias will provide you with a factual overview of a person, place, event, theory, or thing *and* will identify a few well-regarded sources (typically secondary ones, but sometimes also primary) under a heading such as Further Reading or Selected References. So you have at your fingertips both background and several specific works to get your research project launched, a nifty package deal.

In my work with students I occasionally recommend several other kinds of hybrid tools, although general and specialized encyclopedias are by far my top picks. The others are sweeping historical surveys, with different experts responsible for different chapters (such as the *Cambridge History of Medicine*); survey articles, "state of the art" essays, also by experts who write lengthy reviews of the theories and research studies surrounding a complex topic (Bill Maurer's chapter, "The Anthropology of Money," in the 2006 volume of the *Annual Review of Anthropology*); college-level textbooks (Odum and Barrett's *Fundamentals of Ecology*). My favorite type of hybrid tool is the "living encyclopedia," people who have discovered new knowledge or who have taken part in recent social, political, or technological revolutions (not only famous faculty but also local leaders, family friends, and activist relatives fall into this category).

I mention these alternative hybrid tools so you will realize that traditional encyclopedias are not the only game in town when it comes to blending authoritative information with advice on good sources. But I am not going to dwell on them as part of a search strategy.

What about Wikipedia? Like a colorful country fair, Wikipedia offers a mix of accurate, stable exhibits and fantastic sideshows, but instead of depending on farmers and hucksters, Wikipedia's entertainment comes from a motley crowd of self-identified experts. I turn to Wikipedia once or twice a week as a convenience or for some odd fact, but before I rely on it, I always double-check both its assertions and its references. I encourage you to do the same, not just for Wikipedia but for any tool you use or any source on which you base your own conclusions.

◥ MARY'S MAXIM #7: Verify, Verify, Verify

I have listed hybrid tools last because they serve two purposes and—because of that versatility—they belong at the *start* of your search strategy, to which I now return, describing one step at a time. I want you to see how each piece contributes to the whole process and why it is efficient to work through the eight steps in order.

Search Strategy Step 1

Read background information on your research questions in one or more specialized, as opposed to general, encyclopedias.

This is not the first time I've mentioned encyclopedias in this book. By my count, they have come up at least five times before: as a means scholars use to communicate their knowledge; as a location you should identify both in a physical library (where are the encyclopedias shelved?) and on its Web site (what link do I click to get to digital encyclopedias my library provides?); as a help in choosing a topic; as a way to familiarize yourself with key aspects of your topic prior to brainstorming; and as the premier "brand" of hybrid tool. Now they appear again as the first step in a search strategy. I hope that, rather than yawning at this repetition, you will get the message that encyclopedias are vital, the Swiss Army knives of any research project. If you have them handy and know how to use them, you will be in good shape for the adventures ahead.

The reason encyclopedias keep popping up is that the role they play in library research shifts and accelerates in the course of the process. For topic selection and prebrainstorm background you would use a general encyclopedia, such as the *Britannica*, whereas at the start of the search strategy stage you should turn to a specialized, or *subject*, encyclopedia instead. A subject encyclopedia can encompass an entire group of fields (*International Encyclopedia of the Social & Behavioral Sciences*), a single large field (*Encyclopedia of Sociology*), a subspecialty of a field (*Encyclopedia of World Poverty*), or even a sub-subspecialty (*Encyclopedia of Homelessness*). You get the idea. Will there be such a range of focused encyclopedias for all your potential research projects in college? Probably not, but that doesn't matter. The important thing is to identify at least one subject encyclopedia—preferably published within the past half decade—and to mine it for all it's worth: overview articles, key terms and dates, names of pioneers or experts on your topic, statistical tables or illustrations, and (not least) references to significant sources, keeping track in your research log of whatever strikes you and where you saw it.

So the question is, how do you determine what subject encyclopedias exist at your library that will do this essential job? There are two easy ways. One is to ask a reference librarian for advice, and the other is to search your library's online catalog, doing a keyword search that combines a few terms that describe your research questions with the words *encyclopedia* or *dictionary* or *handbook*.

Search Strategy Step 2

Begin to compile several lists (in your research log) and continue this practice throughout the library research process. The most important lists include

a. Relevant terms or phrases for your research, plus synonyms for them;
b. Call numbers you encounter for relevant books;
c. Subject headings you encounter for relevant books and descriptive phrases you encounter in databases;
d. Names of experts who have studied your topic or written about your research questions, and organizations concerned with them;
e. Titles of scholarly journals or topic-focused periodicals that publish in the field(s) you are exploring.

When I discussed the advantages of a research log in chapter 2, I urged you to keep track of both background information you come across in your quest for an interesting topic and your own hunches as you brainstorm. Now you can add detail to those earlier notations because you will start to notice the unique vocabulary, categories, issues, creators, and channels of communication that surround your topic and research questions. What was guesswork at the brainstorming stage will become recurring, reliable guidelines during the search strategy stage.

I think these lists are self-explanatory, and I suggest some additional ones in the boxed chart. As a practical matter, I recommend devoting a separate section in your research log to each of them, so that you don't mix up different types of clues.

A More Complete List of Lists
Every Researcher Should Keep

1. **Keywords** from thinking, brainstorming, background reading, or a thesaurus
2. **Relevant call numbers,** to use for both shelf and online browsing purposes
3. **Subject headings** from the fullest display in an online catalog *and* **subject descriptors** from every relevant article database
4. **Authors and scholars** whose work is repeatedly mentioned by others
5. **Titles of peer-reviewed journals** and popular periodicals
6. **Titles of relevant reference tools** related to the research project
7. **Publishers** that seem to specialize in the field
8. **Institutions, associations, societies, or government agencies** that focus on the area of interest
9. **Dates,** such as the life span of key people, the exact date of a major event, or the publication year of primary sources
10. **Order of the steps** taken to obtain background information and discover sources, including the navigation path leading to electronic resources and the address of useful Web pages

Search Strategy Step 3

Search your own library's online catalog for

a. Specific book sources listed at the end of the encyclopedia articles you have read;

b. Additional book sources your library owns, using the subject heading links attached to the specific book sources you look up;

c. Still more book sources your library owns, using combinations of keywords.

There is a crucial distinction between looking for information or sources that will help answer your research questions, and looking for specific sources others have recommended. In the first case—what I call **scouting**—you don't know what you will come across, but in the second case—what I call **trapping**—you do. Both scouting and trapping occur in every research project, whether the researcher is a novice or a Nobelist. Put another way, it is the difference between asking, *What exists?* and asking, *Where can I get X, a source I already know exists?*

A lead to a specific source (the X in the preceding sentence) can come verbally from your instructor, from the suggested reading list that follows an encyclopedia entry, from the references at the end of an article in a scholarly journal, or from the notes and bibliography in a book by an expert. The point is that some presumably reliable person has supplied you with the author, title, or other identifying characteristics of a source, so that you are then looking for a known item. Every time you search your library's online catalog you should ask yourself which mode you are in, scouting or trapping: do you want to determine what sources your library owns that may be relevant (scouting), or whether your library has a specific book (trapping)? When you engage in more complex research projects in college, such as an honors thesis or a seminar paper, your scouting will also become more complex as you attempt to learn what pertinent sources exist *anywhere,* not just locally. When you identify what seem to be good sources that your library does not own, you will trap them in other ways, for instance, by borrowing them from other libraries, requesting digital scans or photocopies, or traveling to use an archive of unpublished correspondence at another institution.

Search Strategy Step 4

Begin systematic browsing of your library's shelves, looking on the shelves for all the call numbers you have established in step 3.

This discovery technique came up in chapter 2 when I described different ways to settle on a research topic, so I only stress the word *systematic* now. Even though you may need just a handful of printed sources for your research project, resist the temptation to zip into your library's stacks, seize the specific book you came for, and zip back to the circulation desk to check it out. Give yourself a few minutes to see what else is on the same shelf, remembering that discoveries often come from accidental encounters.

MARY'S MAXIM #8:
TAKING TIME WILL SAVE TIME

Search Strategy Step 5

Search relevant indexes and databases to identify specific articles on your topic in both scholarly and popular publications, including newspapers.

Here you'll be scouting and trapping micro sources, articles or chapters by different writers—or, of course, the electronic full-text versions thereof. I go over how to do this in chapter 4. My only caution is that if your topic is recent (for example, an event that happened six months ago), the only sources that exist so far may be newspaper accounts and editorials plus articles in popular periodicals. It may be too soon for books or articles in scholarly journals. Therefore, if you cannot identify books on precisely your topic, don't despair; there may be plenty of sources at the micro (article) level that you can identify through multidisciplinary databases.

Search Strategy Step 6

Skim everything you locate to determine which sources may be the most useful and to get leads to additional specific sources.

Some students feel they must read everything they identify from beginning to end. Not so. At this point in the search strategy you are still shopping for an outfit of good sources, and it is OK—in fact, prudent—to review things quickly, deciding which are keepers, which may be helpful, and which are irrelevant or redundant. One of the two major challenges for all researchers is evaluating sources in light of their research questions. (The other one is integrating sources into their argument and conclusions.) I describe some standard criteria for evaluating sources in chapter 5, but you shouldn't be surprised that it takes practice to spot the features of a source that make it more or less useful for your research. Once you get in the habit of weighing clues, doing so will become second nature for all your future projects.

Search Strategy Step 7

Return to your library's online catalog to find call numbers for the additional books you have identified via footnotes and bibliography entries and to determine if your library subscribes to the periodicals or newspapers for which you now have article references. Track these sources down.

This step sounds repetitious, so is it necessary? You bet it is. Your scouting and trapping activities to this point will have led you more or less in a circle surrounding your ultimate prey: the specific sources that will help you answer your research questions. Once you capture (obtain) them and decide which are most relevant, they in turn will point you to still others. Knowing when to stop searching—when enough is enough—is not always easy. For some assignments you will run out of available sources or time before you run out of leads. For others (and here I'm thinking ahead, toward research projects you may undertake as a college junior or senior), the possibilities will seem infinite and overwhelming. The important thing is not to let yourself become paralyzed.

Remember, anxiety is normal in the research process for both novices and experts. You need to tough it out and continue to apply your mind to the sources you have found. Sooner or later you'll have an epiphany, a moment of insight, about how you can answer your research questions and use your sources to build a compelling argument. The work is not over when that happens, but you will definitely feel less anxious and more in control of your project from then on.

Search Strategy Step 8

Repeat steps 3 through 7 as necessary until you have in hand the variety of sources you imagined when you were brainstorming, conferring at least once with your teacher during the process.

Repeating steps 3 through 7 may not, in fact, be necessary if you've discovered good sources in your first pass, but touching base with your instructor is definitely a smart move. If your hunt for sources has gone well, you will be reassured. If not, your instructor might suggest, for example, a new angle of your research questions to focus on, additional keywords you could try in your searching, a kind of source (say, a diary) you hadn't thought of in your brainstorming, or a different way to work with the sources you already have. It is especially wise to discuss with your instructor the argument (often called a thesis statement) you intend to make and an outline of the points involved. That way you'll get helpful feedback before you have invested a lot of time in preparing your essay or presentation.

What Good Are Fact Tools?

You may have noticed that the search strategy I recommend is missing something: there are no fact tools in any of the steps, just hybrid tools (subject encyclopedias) at the start and the three kinds of finding tools (your library's online catalog, indexes, and bibliographies) later on. The reason should be obvious. By their nature fact tools are ad hoc—sometimes you need them, sometimes you don't. For one research project you may turn frequently to a handbook, chronology, biographical compilation, or bilingual dictionary. For another project, the background information in general and subject encyclopedias may suffice. You can never predict which fact tools you may want or when in the search strategy you may want them, so just keep their existence and variety in mind. When the need arises, you can ask a reference librarian to suggest a good one for the job.

When I speak about a search strategy as a basic recipe, fact tools are the optional ingredients—herbs, spices, seasonings, and so on—that you should have on hand but might not need for any given cooking project. The analogy is not perfect, but you see the point.

About Quantity

Students often ask me how many sources they should identify, locate, and use for a research project. I advise them to check with their professor, but I also share a guideline of my own: try to discover *three times* as many sources as you expect to actually use for your argument. For instance, if your assignment specifies a minimum of two book sources and five articles, at least three of which must be from scholarly journals, then you should aim to come up with at least six book sources and fifteen possible articles, nine of the latter from scholarly journals.

Obviously, this is a rule of thumb, not a rigid formula. The main purpose is to provide your mind, and hence your argument, with choices. After I discuss evaluation in the final chapter, you will have a better idea of how you might choose among sources. But there is also a secondary, practical rationale for the three-times rule. Identifying more sources than you need will serve you well if one or more of them are not available in time for you to use them. You will have backup sources ready without needing to re-create your catalog or database searches, check out more books, or photocopy additional articles. So my message is to scout broadly and trap liberally—that is, acquire more sources than you may in fact employ in your argument.

On to Tactics

The next chapter covers procedures for carrying out the steps in the search strategy: discovering sources in various formats, and both locating and obtaining sources that are not on your library's shelves or available through its databases or the open Internet. To help with these tasks, I suggest how best to phrase questions to reference librarians, whether you contact them in person, by phone, via e-mail, or instant messaging.

4

The Fine Art of Finding Sources

This chapter is on tactics, about how best to find sources to help you answer your research questions. Here I mean *find* in all senses of the word: to identify the existence of sources, to verify the accuracy of citations (if they are incomplete or in conflict with other references you have), to locate the sources you have identified, and then to actually obtain them.

Before we begin, I need to acknowledge two complications. One is that every assignment, project, and set of research questions is unique, not because it has never occurred to anyone before in the history of human curiosity, but because each researcher is unique. The knowledge and the experience you bring to your project differ from your instructor's knowledge and experience, as well as from what your contemporaries may know and have experienced.

The other complication is that the resources you will encounter—especially the combination of tools and sources in any library's collection—are also unique. Furthermore, every researcher must deal with such variables as the location and hours of their library, the availability of reference staff, the extent of remote access to electronic databases, circulation periods for materials, how quickly items can be borrowed from elsewhere, and a whole raft of local policies and procedures. You will find variations even among libraries within a school district, across a public library system, or on the same college campus. I do not try to address every specific circumstance but instead urge you to acquaint yourself with your library's peculiarities during the self-orientation process outlined in chapter 2. If you are ever stumped about how to "translate" the steps in this book to your own setting, you know what to do: ask.

My response to both complications is to be generic when I explain library research tactics, relying on you to figure out how to accomplish each action in your own situation. Every researcher gets stuck sooner or later, so there is no shame in seeking help. The challenge is to communicate clearly about what you have already done and found. I have some "scripts" to assist you when you contact a reference librarian, but the crucial thing is to be specific.

How Far We've Come

Let's review: you've started with a research assignment, settled on an interesting general topic, done some background reading, begun a research log, brainstormed about various aspects of your topic, and chosen at least one research question to investigate. You are also aware of the difference between tools and sources, know that tools come in three "flavors"—fact, finding, and hybrid—and have learned that sources can be primary or secondary depending on how they address your research question. You understand that if you follow a basic search strategy, using finding tools to identify sources, your research process can be thorough and efficient. Lastly, you foresee the need to evaluate sources in the light of each research question, and know that at some point you will have an insight about how all your evidence can fit together in a compelling argument, the story you will ultimately tell your audience.

Until now I have been using the plural phrase *research questions* because most complex projects involve two or more related inquiries. From here on in this chapter, I use the singular, *research question* or just *question,* to avoid grammatical difficulties. You will need to apply each tactic I discuss to each of your questions, and I suggest that you do so concurrently. That is, when you search your library's online catalog to identify secondary (interpretive) book sources on your question A, you might as well do the same for your question B. This not only will save time but will allow you to discover new connections. Perhaps the same expert has written books on both your questions, or perhaps the concept you are exploring originated in another field. Those could be promising leads, or even triggers for your insight.

What Exists? Where Is It?
Is It Any Good?

These are the core concerns of the library research process. No amount of speculation about what information, reference tools, or specific sources might be helpful can replace the actual experience of seeking them. I hope I have convinced you that the preliminary steps in the process are themselves essential, but we're now to the Hunt, where inquiry meets reality. The Hunt has three overlapping phases: determining that sources with certain features exist, obtaining them, and assessing whether or not they really relate to your research question. Logically, all three must occur for you to succeed. If you can't identify the sources you imagined when you brainstormed, if you spot one but can't acquire it in the time you have, or if you recognize that it is not in fact useful, then you need to release it and keep hunting.

 MARY'S MAXIM #9: Expect Complexity

Call to the Hunt

It is important to grasp the difference between scouting (exploring to see what sources there are) and trapping (acquiring them). Both ventures are forms of discovery. When you explore, you don't yet know what relevant tools (fact, finding, and hybrid) and sources (primary and secondary) may exist, so you are trying to identify them. Once you have done so, your aim will be to obtain them, either as physical objects (books or journal articles) or as virtual objects (electronic texts or images). Some finding tools—notably any library's online catalog and quite a few article databases—will help you complete both tasks at the same time: you will learn not only that a helpful source exists but also that it "lives" on a certain shelf in the collection or in digital form behind a hot link. In other cases, you will need to follow a more involved procedure, first deciding that a specific source seems useful, then determining where or how you can get it, then taking the appropriate steps to do so. I return to these maneuvers a bit later, but I want to caution you that—Google and its rivals notwithstanding—you should never count on rounding up all the sources you need for a project simply by surfing the Web and downloading files you come across there. Rarely will you be able to complete a research assignment successfully without moving away from your computer.

↖ MARY'S MAXIM #10: EXERT MIND, MOUSE, AND MUSCLE TOGETHER

The next sections address concepts and methods involved in discovering sources, both how to identify them and how to actually get them. In chapter 5, I discuss ways to judge how well the sources you have collected answer your research question.

Nouns to Know Now: Citation, Reference, Record, and Abstract

I use *citation* and *reference* interchangeably to mean a basic description of a source, whether someone else provides it to you—say, at the end of an entry in a subject encyclopedia—or you provide it to your own readers. The purpose of a citation or reference is to document evidence so that others can, if they like, track it down themselves.

Two related, but more complex, terms I use frequently are *record* and *abstract*. A *record* is information (about a source) that you retrieve from an online catalog or article database. A record can be a bare-bones description—not much more than a citation—or it can offer you valuable clues about the features and content of a source. An abstract, which is part of each item's record in an article database, provides the best help of all: a summary of that source. Whenever you see an abstract, read it *before* you do anything

(continued on next page)

---

else. Why? Because the abstract will state the author's hypothesis, research methods, results, and conclusions, reducing the essence of a long scholarly article to a short paragraph. Then, if the abstract seems promising, you can click the full-text link or take other steps to obtain the article.

Discovering Sources: Theory

It stands to reason that you can't capture sources if you don't know what you're looking for. Likewise, no matter how precise your inquiry is, you will falter if you rely exclusively on your own vocabulary and, as a result, either overlook an essential idea or miss a good source that has a clever title but offers no hint that it can help you.

Veteran researchers and librarians cope with this dilemma by continually switching back and forth between **known-item searching** and **concept searching,** which itself has two variants, **keyword searching** and **assigned-subject searching.** They do known-item searching when they already have a reference to a source they want to trap, and concept searching of both types when they want to scout for sources but do not know of any specific ones. For them, the two approaches are as automatic as inhaling and exhaling, but as a novice you need to realize that sometimes you will be looking for a source recommended by someone else, in the form of a written citation or a spoken suggestion, and other times you will be relying either on your own words, derived from your research question, or on subject terms applied to a source by someone else. Figure 4.1 illustrates the options.

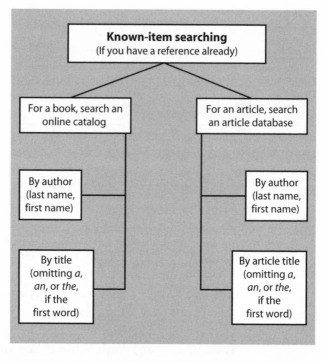

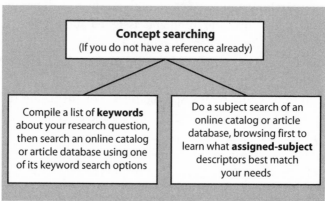

Figure 4.1: Searching for Sources

Note the boxes that show the two kinds of concept searching: **keyword** (using words and phrases *you* think best represent your research question) and **assigned-subject** (using words and phrases *someone else* has already given each source). Assigned subjects go by many names, including subject headings, descriptors, controlled or standardized vocabulary, thesaurus-based terminology, and authorized headings.

Concept searching is not simply a matter of throwing notions from your head into your favorite browser's search box. Terms that come from your thinking, brainstorming, conferring with your instructor, background reading, research log, and fact tools (such as dictionaries) you consult are all necessary, but they are not, alas, sufficient. To do a thorough job of concept searching, you will also need to figure out and use the terminology *which has already been assigned* to sources that might be useful for your research. Who assigns these terms? Catalogers assign them to book sources. Indexers assign them to article sources. The role of catalogers and indexers is to describe sources they add to finding tools so that researchers can retrieve everything relevant.

OK, you say, so how do I guess what words and phrases these strangers have used? And even if I do guess correctly, what payoff do I get from the effort? There are several reassuring answers to those concerns. One is that catalogers and indexers apply standardized vocabulary to sources *they have actually examined,* so the benefit when you search with *their* terms is that you won't miss relevant sources that don't happen to match *your* terms. For instance, you might want material on what you (and most people) call *cars,* but that catalogers and indexers all call *automobiles,* regardless of the actual title of any book or article. Hence, if you search using *automobiles,* you will identify everything your library's catalog and databases have to offer.

Second, the words and phrases that specialists give to sources are easy to discover because they compile them in a list you can view, adding new terms as necessary (SEPTEMBER 11 TERRORIST ATTACKS, 2001) and pointing from synonyms to their "official" term for a concept (ROCKET SHIPS, SEE SPACE VEHICLES). You are already familiar with cross-referencing, as this pointing is called, from telephone books, where alternative spellings of last names appear in the white pages and advice on "correct" terminology is found in the yellow pages (DOCTORS, SEE PHYSICIANS).

Every library's online catalog and most article databases—the exception being some newspaper databases that allow you to search for articles by keywords only—will have a way, usually through an obvious icon or link, for you to scan its internal thesaurus of subject terms, then choose appropriate ones and search them with just a mouse click or two. Taking a minute to browse an online subject thesaurus before you search will help you uncover sources you would otherwise miss if left to your own descriptors. Reference librarians can show you where to find and how to interpret the subject thesaurus that goes with any online catalog or article database.

Third, these professionals take time to analyze each source when they have it in hand, not just for its main content but also for its approach and other features, such as the inclusion of maps or illustrations. For instance, you may be interested only in topic X, and a book may seem from its title to be only about topic Y. If a cataloger has noticed that it contains a significant treatment of X, and has included a detail to that effect in the catalog, your well-constructed search will identify that source.

A fourth and related point is that, after examining a source, a cataloger or indexer will typically give it a *variety* of terms to reflect its intellectual angles. The result is that, in addition to using several keywords to look for one source that will be relevant, you can also look at the description of one relevant source, then use its assigned-subject headings to burrow deeper into the catalog or database to bring more sources to light.

Since this is both the most difficult and the most important point to grasp, here is an example. Let's suppose that your topic concerns censorship of novels in America in the twentieth century, and that your research question is, "How did the Cold War influence censorship activities?" (Recall from the brainstorming checklist in chapter 2 that *how* and *why* research questions are always more interesting than *who, what, when,* or *where* ones, or than those you can answer with just *yes* or *no*.) Your professor has recommended a scholarly book he knows your library owns, by an author named Steinle and with the phrase *In Cold Fear* somewhere in the title.* If you perform a known-item search of your online catalog with those clues, you will see the basic description of the Steinle work, along with its call number. But if you then look at the extended form of the book's description (you may need to click a button labeled "full display," "long view," or the like), you will be astounded to learn that a cataloger has given it *ten* different subject headings, any of which—had you done a keyword search instead of a known-item search in the first place—would also have led you to this source. Since each of the ten subject

---

*Pamela Hunt Steinle, *In Cold Fear: The* Catcher in the Rye *Censorship Controversies and Postwar American Character* (Columbus: Ohio State University Press, 2000).

headings is a hot link, all you need to do to discover more book sources related to your question is to click sequentially on those that look most helpful, for instance, FICTION—CENSORSHIP—UNITED STATES, or SALINGER, J. D. (JEROME DAVID), 1919—CENSORSHIP.

Last, online catalogs—and quite a few article databases—use the *same* subject headings, so you will likely need to search only a handful of assigned terms to identify useful sources. I encourage you to use your research log to keep track of the most relevant subject headings you discover in each catalog or database, so you can refer to them and re-search with them elsewhere in the future. To get the biggest research bang for the buck, you should make use of multiple terms, both keywords from your thinking and subject descriptors that specialists have assigned to sources.

Absolutely everything I've said in the last few pages can be summarized by another maxim.

MARY'S MAXIM #11: ONE GOOD THING LEADS TO ANOTHER

Where you begin searching is never as important as recognizing which clues you already have and how to follow them in your quest for sources. The ratio of known-item searching to concept searching will vary with each research project, but generally you will do a smattering of known-item searching at the start (looking for sources mentioned at the end of an encyclopedia entry, for instance), followed by a lot of concept searching of both types (keyword and assigned-term), then more known-item searching toward the end of your strategy as you read and reflect and notice other intriguing sources experts have mentioned.

Discovering Sources: Overview of Approaches

There are three principal and interconnected tactics involved in the search for sources. They are

Tactic 1.   Using keywords to search a library's online catalog or an article database;

Tactic 2.   Using "givens"—that is, assigned-subject descriptors—to literally re-search the same online catalog or article database;

Tactic 3.   Using a reference to a specific book or article to locate and obtain it.

Supporting these tactics are three others:

Tactic 4.   Verifying details about a source;

Tactic 5.   Browsing the shelf where a relevant book source is;

Tactic 6.   Using the documentation (bibliography and notes) of scholarly (secondary) sources you come across to lead you to others.

These six methods are interdependent, but I find that starting with terms the researcher brings to the task is always more gratifying, and usually faster, than other approaches. In addition, keyword-first searching is likely to reveal several recent sources that are locally and readily available, either on a shelf or online.

Unless I note otherwise, the following explanation applies to *both* online catalog searching (which leads to books) *and* database searching (which leads to articles of various types).

Tactic 1: Discovering Sources—
Keyword Approach

Keywords are the vocabulary that surrounds your research question. Keywords come from various places, most commonly from your research assignment itself, your background reading (in a hybrid tool), conferring with your teacher, thinking about your topic and research question, brainstorming with friends, and looking up words in a dictionary or thesaurus (both fact tools). If your research is likely to involve sources in a foreign language—and assuming you are at least moderately fluent in it—then you will need to list keywords in both English and the other language(s).

I confess that when I meet with a student to help identify sources that address their research question, we often miss important terms on the first try. That's inevitable, I think, given the bounty of English vocabulary and our human tendency to type whatever words occur to us in any search box we see. Although you may trust Google to read your mind and come up with useful Web links, that is not the best technique for searching either online catalogs or article databases. Rather, this problem solves itself because even the most basic keyword search will quickly reveal additional terms you can use in other searches to achieve more precise results. These additional terms turn up in the titles, assigned-subject descriptors, contents listings, and abstracts of the items you retrieve from even the "dumbest," most spontaneous initial search. To harness the expansive power of keyword searching, you just need to stay alert as you explore, remain open to different ways of stating your research question, and be ready to jot down new ideas for future use.

Here is an example. Let's say you are asking to what extent eating disorders caused by peer pressure may correlate with academic performance in college. Together we decide the question involves concepts related to medicine, education, and age. So we jot down the keywords we intend to use in three columns, like this:

Medical Keywords	Education Keywords	Age Keywords
eating disorders	achievement	college students
anorexia	success	teenagers
bulimia		young adults
obesity		

Then, because you want to find periodical articles first, we construct a keyword search in a multidisciplinary database that looks like this:

eating disorders OR anorexia OR bulimia OR obesity

AND

achievement OR success

AND

college students OR teenagers OR young adults

The three sets of concepts can, of course, be in any order; the results of your search will be the same. I am writing the connecting words *or* and *and* in capital letters just so the logic will be clear, although most online catalogs and databases are not case sensitive, meaning you can enter your keywords either way.

Only after we experiment for a few minutes and scrutinize our results does it dawn on us that we would probably get better results if we include the words **weight** and **health** in the first group of keywords, **adolescents** and **youth** in the third group, and if we *avoid* the terms **parents** or **family**. And indeed that's what happens. The need to go back and redo searches is a common experience—in fact, this sort of tinkering will help you gauge the number of possible sources so you can decide whether to expand or narrow your next search—but you can minimize your effort if you start with a longer list of keywords. Whenever and however you discover additional relevant keywords, be sure to write them in your research log so that they will be handy throughout the rest of your strategy.

Now let's fine-tune that same example. Rewritten in the format common to most catalogs and databases, with the additional keywords, it becomes

> (**"eating disorder*"** OR **anorexi*** OR **bulimi***
> OR **weight*** OR **health***)
> **AND**
> (**achieve*** OR **success***)
> **AND**
> (**"college student*"** OR **teen*** OR **"young adult*"**
> OR **youth** OR **adolescen***)
> **NOT**
> (**parent*** or **famil***)

This looks weird, I grant you, so let me explain what's going on. The parentheses around the different concept groups are there to keep each set of synonyms together. If a source concerns either anorexia or bulimia or any of the other terms in that group, you would be interested in it—provided it *also* concerns either achievement or success, *plus* any one of the key ideas in the third group, but not either of the terms in the fourth group. This is an unusually complex case, but I want to point out what's possible. The logic is mix-and-match because you don't know what you will turn up, so you can't search for a specific author or book title. (This would also be true if we were trying a keyword search in an article database instead of a library's online catalog.) You can consider this a fishing expedition, if you like, and you will usually catch some relevant sources quickly. But even if you don't, keep in mind that negative results—for example, if you don't find any book sources about your research question—are themselves meaningful, if frustrating. In fact, graduate students and other advanced researchers will often breathe a sigh of relief when they do *not* turn up books on their topic because they want to be the first to write one, or they realize that their research question is cutting edge and suspect that any sources that exist would be very recent articles in scholarly journals.

There are two major reasons your search may not yield results. One is that your research question may not yet have been treated in a book-length publication (for instance, it could be too current or local for such an extended study). The other reason is that the library whose online catalog you are searching may not have books in its collection related to your research question, or to the larger topic surrounding it. In either case, you will usually discover articles about it in short order as you continue your search strategy. Don't be discouraged when nothing emerges from a library's online catalog on your first try. Instead, give some thought to the keywords and logic you used, confer with a reference librarian, make a note about what you did in your research log, and keep trucking.

As to the quotation marks around and the asterisks (aka stars) following some of the keywords: quotation marks are a traditional way to make words stick together as a phrase, and an asterisk is the most common "wildcard" symbol to

---

Truncation: The Researcher's Friend

The formal term for using symbols to represent letters is *truncation,* which simply means to cut something short. It is indeed a shortcut because, used thoughtfully in an online catalog or article database search, it saves time and keystrokes. However, if you don't stop and think before you truncate keywords, you will get some bizarre results. For example, entering *war** when you want sources about either wars or warriors will also yield sources about warblers, wardrobes, and warranties. I find this amusing (briefly) when it happens to me, but then I redo my search to avoid such false hits, as they are called.

---

indicate that you want all the variants of a word. Rather than type *teen, teen's, teens, teens', teenage, teenager, teenager's, teenagers,* and *teenagers',* just *teen** will do the job, allowing you to retrieve online catalog or article database records that include any form of the root word. Nine keywords reduced to one is a real bargain.

Here's the rub: depending on the design of whatever electronic finding tool you are searching, you may not need to put quotation marks around phrases, asterisks at the end of terms to truncate them, or logical connectors to specify how your keywords relate to each other (typing *or* between synonyms, *and* to combine groups, *not* if you ever want to exclude a concept). Why? Because most offer an advanced (sometimes called a guided) search screen where you can enter your keywords in multiple boxes and use menus or checkmarks to indicate how you want them to be combined. My advice to people who want to do keyword searching—

and this is everyone sooner or later—is to find and use the advanced search option in each catalog or database they try. You don't need to fill in more than one box or use all the possible connectors, but these features are there if you want them. Another benefit of working with a tool's advanced search screen is that you will be better able to see why you got puzzling results and how you can fine-tune your search. And don't be surprised to find that each search interface has its own quirks—most often the use of a truncation symbol other than, or in addition to, the asterisk, for instance, *?*, *!*, *#*, *&*, or *$* (go figure). Remember

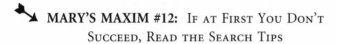

MARY'S MAXIM #12: IF AT FIRST YOU DON'T SUCCEED, READ THE SEARCH TIPS

George Boole and John Venn

Here is the place to mention two British thinkers, George Boole (1815–1864) and John Venn (1834–1923), whose work has a direct bearing on the library research process. Boole is known for his formulation of various laws of reasoning that we use to combine keywords in an online catalog or article database search. The example I used previously, of constructing a search about adolescent weight and college success, illustrates Boolean logic in that keywords or phrases that are either synonymous or related to one aspect of the research question are strung together with the operator *or*, while groups of terms that qualify one another are connected with *and*, and concepts to exclude are indicated with *not*.

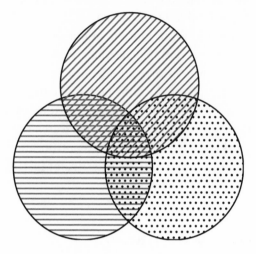

Figure 4.2: Venn Diagram

The important, and difficult, thing to understand is that Boolean logic is the *opposite* of addition and subtraction in arithmetic. **When you add concepts to one another in a Boolean search (using the connector *and*), you are *reducing* the number of results you will get from a catalog or database because you are being more precise about what you want.** Fortunately, many Web browsers and finding tools provide ways—usually on their advanced search option—to help people enter the logic they want via menus or boxes with labels such as "any of these [keywords]," "all of these," "none of these," and "exact phrase." Also fortunately, we have John Venn's simple diagram that uses overlapping circles to represent, in this instance, three concept groups, their intersection being the relatively small but relevant set of sources one wants.

Tinkering with Searches

Boolean logic and a Venn diagram will help you formulate your keyword searching, but often you will want to sort or sift your results. Most online catalogs or article databases will display items alphabetically (by author or title), chronologically (typically with the most recently published source listed first), or by relevance (calculated by a hidden rule that weights the key terms you entered). Somewhere on the screen near the top of the display will be a way to change the sorting order. It's a function worth finding, but even more useful is the ability to screen your results by one or more factors. For instance, you might want to retrieve sources published between 1996 and 2000, or ones only in English, or (in an article database) album reviews rather than biographies of the performer. You can apply any of these criteria—singly or in combination—in most electronic finding tools, but you may need to look carefully at the display screen, read the online help text, or confer with a reference librarian to determine how to do this. Look especially for links labeled *modify, refine, revise,* or *qualify.*

Here I want to comment on the worst and the best choices you can make as you search. The worst one is to restrict your search results to items linked to full text (either basic HTML format or a PDF image) in *that* catalog or database. I realize that convenience and deadline pressures make this an extremely enticing approach, but it is also an intellectually limiting one. You will end up suppressing relevant sources you would (and should) want to consider for your research, and which may be readily available in *another* database you have access to, or in another format in your own library. My advice always is

➤ MARY'S MAXIM #13:
Don't Settle for What's Handy

The best search choice, assuming you want articles written by experts—as opposed to popular or journalistic treatments of your topic—is to click the tab or icon provided by most databases that allows you to target your results to scholarly articles. If the way to do this is not obvious, then either explore the help link within the tool or ask a librarian to show you where this powerful option is lurking.

My own preference is to search in two stages, first concentrating on my keywords and Boolean logic, and then, after I see the number and nature of my results, deciding whether and how to adjust my variables. I'd much rather have thousands of hits and the satisfaction of winnowing the total down to a dozen really relevant ones than do a highly restricted search and have nothing to show for it.

Tactic 2: Discovering Sources—
Assigned-Subject Approach

I've already explained that the two "flavors" of concept searching are keyword and assigned-subject, and that the former uses your own terms to describe your topic or research question, whereas the latter relies on uniform terminology applied to each source by the people who create a finding tool. It follows that before you can benefit from the assigned-subject method of searching, you need to figure out what that uniform terminology is. This sounds like a bureaucratic runaround, but it's not. You actually have three ways to figure this out, all literally at your fingertips:

1. Start with a source you already know is relevant, because you've examined it or someone has recommended it to you. Look it up in the library's online catalog (if it's a book) or in an article database (if it's an article). Once you are looking at the record describing the source, find a button or link on the screen that will display the maximum information about it. Typically, the button or link will be labeled "full display," "complete record," "more information," or something similar. If you don't see it right away, ask a reference librarian how to drill down for this detail. When you do, along with notes on other facets of the source (for instance, indicating it contains maps or is a reprint of an earlier publication) will be links to its subject descriptors. Click on one that seems relevant, and it will lead you to similar sources. (There are two exceptions to this procedure: if you start with a work of literature—a novel, a short story, a play, or a poem—or if you start with a newspaper article. This is because many databases do not assign subject descriptors to such primary sources.)

2. Do a keyword search in the catalog or database, making it as simple or complex as necessary. Look at the list of hits for a source that definitely concerns your research question. (My own rule of thumb is to scroll through no more than two screens of results, and if I do not see anything relevant, I reformulate my search.) Then view that source's description in its fullest form and, as when you start with a known item, exploit its subject descriptors to take you to other useful sources. A nice, if slightly spooky, feature of some article databases is that they attempt to second-guess what you have in mind, suggesting subject descriptors and combinations somewhere on the screen when they display the results of your search.

3. Confront a finding tool head-on to make it yield its list of assigned-subject terms. If you want to identify books, go to the online catalog's main search screen and figure out how to do a subject search, probably by clicking that choice. Enter what *you* think is the most logical descriptor for your topic (for instance, just PUERTO RICO). This tactic is an open sesame command that will reveal the otherwise-hidden thesaurus. You will see a display of all the assigned-subject terms, in alphabetical order, that start with whatever word or phrase you entered. For example, PUERTO RICO—EMIGRATION AND IMMIGRATION, PUERTO RICO—FOREIGN RELATIONS—UNITED STATES, or PUERTO RICO—HISTORY—AUTONOMY AND INDEPENDENCE MOVEMENTS.

You will also likely encounter note icons next to certain entries. These are a big help to any researcher, so don't ignore them. The text behind such an icon will tell you what that term means and may point you to broader, narrower, or related subject headings used in the catalog. For instance, if you start with the subject pollution, you will see the explanation, "Here are entered works on the condition resulting from the action of environmental contaminants. Works on the substances which contaminate or degrade the environment are entered under POLLUTANTS," plus suggestions for more specific subject headings to search such as ELECTRIC POWER-PLANTS—ENVIRONMENTAL ASPECTS, GROUNDWATER POLLUTION, or HAZARDOUS WASTES. Since these alternatives will be links, you can follow any one of them with just another mouse click and quickly arrive at what you are seeking.

If, instead of a book, you want articles on your research question from scholarly journals, popular periodicals, news

About Serials and Peer Review

The word *serial* pops up frequently in library research. It is the umbrella term for a publication that contains articles, appears more or less on a predictable schedule, and is sold to libraries and individuals via subscription. (The equivalent word to describe a book publication, typically one volume devoted to a single topic, is *monograph*.) The most common types of serials are magazines, newsmagazines, newspapers, periodicals, and scholarly journals. Scholarly journals are those intended for a specialist audience—you will seldom find issues at a newsstand—and that publish what are called peer-reviewed articles, meaning each contribution is evaluated by a panel of experts prior to publication. The adjectives *academic, juried, peer-reviewed, refereed,* and *scholarly* are used interchangeably to indicate the nature of an entire journal and its individual articles. Most article databases allow you to restrict your search results to peer-reviewed articles, but if you are ever unsure about a journal's character, you can check *Ulrich's Periodicals Directory* (a fact tool available online or in print in every library). You might also want to revisit the discussion of peer review in chapter 1.

magazines, or newspapers, then you should carefully examine the first search screen that appears, looking for labels such as *browse, subjects, index,* or *thesaurus.* These labels may appear next to an icon, a link, a button, or a box, but regardless of the wording or screen design, their function is to lead you down into a researcher's gold mine, the assigned vocabulary used in that database. If you don't see any such label on the database's opening screen, then look for the advanced search option—it may also be called a guided or fielded or complex search—which will present you with several choices, among which will be a route to the assigned-subject terms. Typically, you can search or scroll through a list, then select the term you want and, with a single click, have it appear in the appropriate search box without your having to copy and paste it there.

Tactic 3: Discovering Sources— Known-Item Approach

At several points in every project, you will discover leads to specific sources you want to obtain. Sometimes the lead will provide the source instantly, as when your instructor both suggests a good book or article and offers to lend you her personal copy for a few days, or when one entry in an encyclopedia refers you to another one. Other times you may discover the lead on your own in an online catalog or article database, or on a Web site and find a link right on the screen to the full text.

Unfortunately, you cannot rely on effortless techniques alone to get you through an entire research project, especially if you expect to need a wide variety of sources in different physical formats, created over decades or centuries. If you do, the work you produce will be a holey mess because you will miss important information and points of view. So whenever you identify a source you would like to examine, but all you have is a description—from a footnote, bibliographic citation, reference tool, offhand mention in a newspaper story, or your professor's hazy recollection that "a few years ago, Jones published an important paper on your topic"—you need to take action. First, determine whether the source in question is a whole book, a chapter in a collection or anthology, an article, or something else. Then here's what to do, in table form. Note that the steps in the right column are what you should do to obtain any source, regardless of how you identified it.

If it's a whole book	Use the library's online catalog to search for the book by author (last name first) or title (omit the initial articles *A, An, The*). If the title is long, you can usually enter just the first few words, for instance, UNITED STATES OF EUROPE. If the book appears in the catalog, note its location, call number, and status. Assuming it is available, find out where it is shelved. Go there and retrieve it, being alert for other useful sources on the same or adjacent shelves. If the book does not appear in the online catalog, do another type of search. For example, if you started with a title search, do an author search on the second try. If the book still doesn't turn up, or if the library owns it but it happens to be checked out or missing, confer immediately with a librarian about what you can do to obtain it. Keep in mind that you may need to go to another library to get an item, especially if what you want is unpublished or rare. For other things, ask about your library's interlibrary loan service. If you are eligible

(continued on next page)

and have a week or so to wait, this is
an excellent way to borrow a book from
elsewhere—or, in the case of an article, obtain a photocopy or digital version you can
keep.

If it's a chapter
in a collection
or anthology

Use the library's online catalog to search for
the *book,* by either editor's name (do an
author search) or book title. Do not attempt
to search for the chapter's actual author
or the chapter title, because in most cases
you will not find it. Follow the same steps
as above in order to obtain it.

If it's an article

Show a reference librarian the most complete information you have. Get advice
about whether the library has a database that
is likely to provide the article's full text. If
so, connect to that database and search
by the title of the article (omitting any initial
article) or by the article author (last name
first). If the librarian's opinion is that the
article is not available electronically in a
database, you can try Google Scholar, but
the best bet is usually to search the online
catalog under the title of the magazine,
periodical, journal, or newspaper. If you find
the publication in the catalog, look carefully at the description to see whether the
library owns the year, volume, and precise
issue in which the article appeared. If so,
note the physical format (bound volume or
microform), location, and call number you

(continued on next page)

	need to retrieve the article. Find out how you can make a photocopy of the article, because most libraries do not circulate bound or microform serials.
If it's something else, or you're not sure what it is	Take all the information you have and consult with a reference librarian. (You may be able to do this via a chat service, e-mail, or phone, but it's often best if you examine all the clues together in person.)

Tactic 4: Discovering Sources—Verification

Following a lead someone else has suggested sounds like a no-brainer, and it is—but only about half the time. Experts are human and humans get details wrong, whether citing sources in print or recommending them in conversation. If I had a brick for every incomplete, inverted, misremembered, or misunderstood citation I have ever encountered, I could rebuild the Tower of Babel. Whenever a reference to a source you'd like to use doesn't seem right—for instance, if when you go to the shelf for the bound volume of a periodical containing an article you want, the year and volume in your reference don't match—do not waste time. You can attempt to untangle it on your own by doing a keyword search in the online catalog or an article database, using what you think are the most distinctive and reliable parts of the reference.

As an alternative, you can go to the reference desk and ask a librarian to verify the citation. This is no different than getting a second medical opinion: the librarian will use various tools, perhaps electronic and perhaps not, to substantiate the

---

Detective Work

Suppose the information you have, and which doesn't seem right, is to a book by William Applebaum with the title *The Scientific Foundation of Revolution*. You could try various combinations of these givens—the fewer terms in each search, the better—using the advanced keyword option in the library's online catalog. Eventually just entering the search APPLEBAUM and SCIEN* would get you to the correct information, a book by Wilbur (not William) Applebaum with the title *The Scientific Revolution and the Foundations of Modern Science*. I am often grateful that you can use the name of the publisher, if you have it, in a keyword search, and even just the *first* name of a person if you're not sure about the last name.

---

information you have. Almost always, it will turn out that an important element of the citation you were given is missing or erroneous or garbled. (Sometimes the problem may be your own fault, especially if you've copied the reference down without asking your informant how to spell an author's name.) Once you have a verified, accurate citation, take the relevant step from the table above to acquire the item.

What You'd Like to Know (and can't figure out on your own)	Example of How to Ask a Reference Librarian about It (Be ready to explain what you have already tried.)
Background information on your general topic	Can you recommend a subject encyclopedia that deals with [your topic]?

What You'd Like to Know (and can't figure out on your own)	Example of How to Ask a Reference Librarian about It (Be ready to explain what you have already tried.)
Where is the best place to enter a keyword search	How do I get to the advanced search screen [in an online catalog or article database]?
What subject headings to search in your library's online catalog	How can I tell what subject headings to use in the catalog for [your topic]?
Where to identify articles on your topic	What database would you suggest for popular and scholarly articles about [your topic]? Does it include newspaper articles, or is there a different database for those?
What subject descriptors to search in an article database	Does [name of database] have a list of subject descriptors I can browse? If so, how do I get to it?
How to reduce your search results	Is there a way to adjust my search [in an online catalog or article database] by language, date, or whether the articles are peer reviewed?
How to increase your search results	Since I'm not finding enough sources, what ways would you suggest to broaden my search?
How you can tell from your search hits whether a book or article might be useful for your research	How can I see more information about [a book or article]? What clues can help me evaluate it? How could I find a review of it?"

(continued on next page)

What You'd Like to Know (and can't figure out on your own)	Example of How to Ask a Reference Librarian about It (Be ready to explain what you have already tried.)
How to obtain an article you have identified but that does not have a link to the full text	Please show me how to locate [this specific article for which you have a citation].
If the library has a specific issue of a periodical or newspaper	How can I determine the library's holdings of [name of the periodical or newspaper]?
Whether a reference you found in a bibliography or footnote is correct	I'd like help verifying [this reference].
What to do if a book or bound volume of a periodical is not on the shelf	I can't find [the item with this call number] where it belongs. Can a library staff member double-check?
What to do if a book is checked out or missing, according to the online catalog	What is the best way to obtain [a specific book before my deadline]?
How you obtain a book or article your library does not own	Is it possible to get [a book or article] from another library [within the time I have to complete my research]?
What other sources the library may have related to your topic	I have already explored the online catalog and [name of article database(s)]. What other approaches would you suggest for sources on [my topic]? Are there relevant materials in special collections or in nonprint formats that the library owns?

Tactic 5: Discovering Sources—Browsing

In chapter 2 I described browsing as one way to decide on a research topic and I have alluded to this method several times since. Smart browsing in the book stacks complements wise concept searching in an online catalog. Both approaches allow you to discover several relevant sources at once, approaching them from different angles. Think of a book as a house. It has just one address (call number), where it sits on a street (shelf) next to other books in the same intellectual neighborhood (general subject). Usually a book has several inhabitants (the different themes it treats). You may ultimately want to meet just one person in one house on the street, but first you need to get there, so you're open to any route: directions to the neighborhood, a street name, an exact address, a list of inhabitants, or the name of someone in particular. I'll end this metaphor with

▲ **MARY'S MAXIM #14:** CURIOSITY
BEGETS SERENDIPITY

The best time to browse is all the time. Do not consider it a one-shot step in the library research process, but take every opportunity to examine the book sources you identify and whatever else lives nearby. I've already mentioned features to consider in any book you handle, but I want to reiterate the importance of a bibliography, the roundup of sources the author has used. The ideal bibliography—whether in a scholarly book or appended to a peer-reviewed article—is one that is annotated (saying why each item was helpful to the writer), fairly recent, and organized thematically, so that the reader does not have to skim pages of citations in alphabetical, but not meaningful, order.

Tactic 6: Discovering Sources—Backtracking

This is the final method I want to cover for unearthing relevant sources. It is sometimes called footnote stalking, but I prefer the term *backtracking*. I do not mean this in the sense of repeating something you've already done, but in the sense of looking back at significant sources that scholars with research questions similar to yours have found helpful. How will you determine what those significant sources are? The best way is to browse the bibliographies in books, or in peer-reviewed articles, that you have already identified and obtained.

Let's say you have in hand a book or scholarly article that seems extremely valuable for your project. It might be so for any number of reasons—the way the authors frame the issues, their overview of previous research, the primary sources or methodology they use, the data they report, their interpretation of what they found, illustrations or figures they include, how they organize their argument, and so on. To take full advantage of this central book or article, look carefully at *its* list of works cited to see what sources the writers used. Inevitably, one or more of their citations will jump out at you, providing a new (to you) known item you can pursue, which will in turn lead you to still others. This is what I mean by backtracking, relying on the judgment of experts to point you to sources they esteem.

There are still other discovery techniques, such as tapping into the communication channels of experts or doing something called citation searching to determine the influence of a known item on later thinking in a field. Such methods, while crucial to advanced researchers, are outside the scope of this book.

What if nothing works? you ask. *What do I do if, at any stage or after trying every one of these methods, I still fail to identify relevant sources or I cannot obtain the ones I want?* This fear, the elephant in the classroom, is unfounded for 95 percent of undergraduate research projects. Chances are that if you're frustrated, adjusting or rethinking just one element of your research approach will solve the problem. Suppose your project concerns the barbarian invasions of Europe, that you have decided to focus on Attila the Hun, and that your research question is, "How did he assess his own career?" But alas, you can't identify the ideal primary source you want to answer that question: his memoirs (in English). So you confer with a reference librarian who recommends reading biographical entries on Attila in certain hybrid and fact tools. When you do that you realize that Attila left no writings and that, in any case, fifth-century conquerors were illiterate. However, you also discover, from the references provided by these tools and your library's catalog and article databases, that there are many sources in English about Attila's exploits and influence, so you wisely decide to use these instead as the next best thing. Seek advice and the elephant will vanish.

You may be worried that research that requires using sources is not only complicated but also endless. The complexity will seem less daunting and more interesting as you proceed through the process. You will start to see patterns and references from different people to the *same* major events, issues, or earlier thinkers. You will become more comfortable moving from keyword to assigned-subject concept searching and from either of these back and forth to

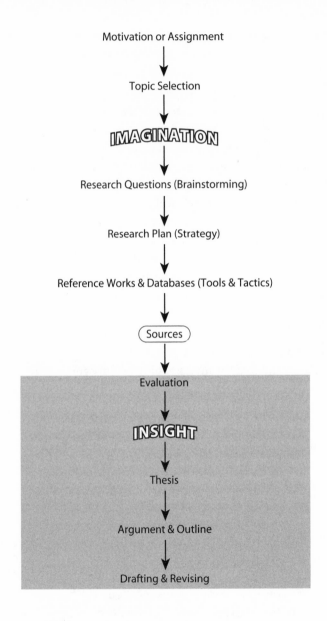

Figure 4.3: Diagram of the Library Research Process

known-item searching. You will get a better idea of what hybrid, fact, and finding tools exist in your own library, and how to obtain the sources you identify, either physically or electronically. In short, your confidence is going to shoot up, and no future research project—regardless of its topic of intricacy—will seem so hard. You may still be a novice, but one with enough experience to know your options.

What about the endless part? Due dates always help, the need to stop scouting and trapping sources and start weaving them into your own argument and presentation. More important than a deadline, however, are the remaining components of the research process: insight and evaluation. As a bridge to the next and final chapter, I present the research flowchart yet again on page 124, shading the elements I have yet to discuss.

5

Insight, Evaluation, Argument,
and Beyond

At the start of the library research process, as you gather
background information on your chosen topic, brainstorm
about it, and begin to discover and review sources, it is your
initial idea—expressed as a research question—that keeps
you moving forward. It's too soon to know where your
inquiry will lead, so you need patience and faith. Provided
you keep working and thinking, you will have an unpredictable flash of insight that will transform how you view
your topic. Your interesting, but probably vague, notion will
suddenly become the germ of a compelling, supportable,
and clear argument. This is your "Aha!" moment, the key to
the case you will ultimately make. Before that point, you can
be guided by a general research *proposal* (whether or not you
have formally written one), which is the equivalent of a
hypothesis in science, a hunch before the facts arrive. Only
after your insight can you write a *thesis,* one true sentence*
that explains your insight and that you can craft into an
argument.

Faculty understand insight, the evolution from idea-
glimmer to idea-glow, because they have gone through the
research process themselves. Unfortunately, their assign-

---

*Ernest Hemingway's phrase from *A Moveable Feast* (New York: Charles Scribner's
Sons, 1964), 12.

ments sometimes rush or confuse things. When a professor says on Monday, "Pick a topic for your term paper and turn in a thesis statement on Friday," or, "Read some background on any issue in medical ethics and present your focus to the class at the next session," he or she is trying to help students jump-start the research process. This is a commendable motive, but it has an unrealistic aim because students will not have enough time to explore and reflect. When this happens to you—it probably has and definitely will—don't be fazed. Instead, concentrate on what the instructor really wants: a preliminary idea about a topic you find interesting, not a commitment cast in stone.

Insight feels terrific; it is a peak intellectual experience to recognize how your research question can be answered convincingly using the sources you have discovered, together with your own ingenuity. Side effects of insight include the urge to stop working and the desire to push on and finish the project immediately. Both reactions are natural, but what you should do instead is take a deep breath, begin to sketch the logic of your paper or presentation, and decide what *additional* types of sources you need to make your argument. Then go after those. Channel the momentum you gain from insight into the remaining stages of the research process: evaluating sources and securing a few more if necessary, articulating your argument and outlining it, and preparing your final "output," from draft to revision. Research projects do move faster following insight, but nonetheless there is Mary's Maxim #15.

◢ MARY'S MAXIM #15: GIVE YOUR
ARGUMENT TIME TO MATURE

Evaluation: Why?

The unexamined life is not worth living, said Socrates.* So too, the unexamined source is not worth finding. When it comes to the library research process, this means you need to judge tools and sources as you go and expect to modify your thoughts, your subsequent steps, and sometimes even your research question, based on your judgments. Here is the basic search strategy, in condensed and slightly reworded form, from chapter 3. Notice how every step involves judgment.

1. Read background information on your research question in one or more specialized encyclopedias.
2. Begin to compile several lists (in your research log) and continue this practice throughout the library research process.
3. Search your own library's online catalog for books you already know about and ones that result from keyword and assigned-subject searches.
4. Begin systematic browsing of your library's shelves, looking on the shelves for all the call numbers you have established in step 3.
5. Search relevant indexes and databases to identify specific articles on your topic in both scholarly and popular publications, including newspapers.
6. Skim everything you locate to determine which sources may be the most useful and to get leads to additional specific sources.

*Plato *Apology* 38a.

7. Return to your library's online catalog to find call numbers for the additional books you have identified and to determine if your library subscribes to the periodicals or newspapers for which you now have article references. Track these sources down.
8. Repeat steps 3 through 7 as necessary until you have found the variety of sources you imagined when you were brainstorming, conferring at least once with your instructor during the process.

The purpose of thinking critically about each aspect of the research process is twofold. First, you can better choose and employ reference tools as you see what sources you are— and are not—uncovering. Second, you can determine as early as possible how a specific source may fit into your future presentation. It is impossible to know the final shape of a project before your insight, and even afterward you will want to scout for a few more "missing" sources to further your argument. Nonetheless, you shouldn't separate the act of finding sources, in every sense of the phrase, from the act of evaluating them. If you do, desperation will set in when you realize, with no time to spare, that the sources you have in hand do not support the argument you have in your head. Then you might as well skip research altogether and write an editorial or debate script concocted from your own beliefs. Far better to weed the hopeless sources from the helpful ones along the way.

Argument Revisited

Let me return to argument, a concept I introduced in chapter 2. In an academic setting—as opposed to a political or interpersonal one—an argument is written or spoken reasoning about an insight, the result of both investigation and analysis, with the goal of persuasion. The library research process involves argument at three overlapping stages:

- Your initial idea about your topic is a sort of embryo argument that will develop as you work through the process.
- The sources you discover, whatever their type and format, provide their creators' arguments.
- Following your insight, you will construct your own detailed argument, based partly on your sources and partly on how you answer your research question.

A caution: if your argument centers on just two opposing aspects of your topic—viewpoints you are examining and trying to reconcile—you should avoid posing it in an either/or manner. A compilation of the pros and cons of anything, however fascinating the issue, quickly bores or irks an audience. If you can express all you have to say in a table or bulleted list, then you have not developed an argument; you have generated an inventory. In other words, the ideal argument emerging from your research should combine sources and insight in a complex way that includes at least a pinch of your personality.

Argument versus Outline

Be careful not to confuse your argument with your outline. Most researchers draw some sort of diagram for themselves to organize the points they want to make, the logic they will use to connect those points, and the sources or research findings they intend to discuss. You will want to do the same as you near the end of your search strategy and start thinking ahead about how best to lay out your insight and conclusions. A traditional outline with numbers, letters, and indentions to show relationships may work well for one person, while a concept map with arrows, or a doodle on a napkin, may suffice for someone else. The form doesn't matter, but the function does. An outline's function is to guide the *writer*. The argument itself is to guide the *reader*. Both need to be clear, but only an argument needs to convince.

Guidelines for Evaluating Sources

You cannot evaluate your sources in the abstract, but only with an end in view—that is, in the context of the argument you are devising. You need to consider each source in relation to (a) your general topic, (b) your research question, (c) your insight once it happens, and (d) how you might use it, that is, the balance or variety or voice it can lend your presentation. You might imagine a large grid with all these factors as column headings and each source you weigh in a row down the side. I don't recommend actually charting your assessment, however, unless this approach appeals to you or you are dealing with dozens of sources and want to rate them on a scale. What I do recommend is on-the-spot triage: making a quick decision when you first encounter a source, whether on a shelf, in a periodical issue you are flipping through, or as you scroll through search results on a computer screen. Elements to consider are the first and last chapters or sections of a source, its table of contents and index (if it has those components, look for your own key terms), its bibliography, and whether it includes graphs or pictures you can use as evidence in your own work. Because of the potential value of photos, maps, and other images, give yourself a minute or two to examine books written in languages you can't read. Their illustrations may supply an angle you are otherwise lacking.

If something seems to have little or no relevance to your research, just move on. This is Level III triage: the source is dead on arrival in your mind, so you don't need to waste time and energy on it.

Level II triage is when you think something has possibilities—for example, as a theoretical lens through which you can view your primary source, as a corroborating or dissenting opinion, or as social context for your topic. Hence you should spend more time to explore it. Take notes about it in your research log, including your quality judgment about the source; the role you foresee for it in your argument; an *exact* transcription, with the precise page reference, of any quotes that strike you; and any leads, especially key terms and citations to other sources, it provides. Make sure you have a complete citation to it so you can readily add it to your list of works cited. Or, if you obtain the full text of an article from a database, be sure to record the name of the database and the date you performed the search because most bibliographic styles require this information.

Lastly, if you decide a source will be central to your argument, then assign it to Level I triage, where close attention on your part will yield a high payoff. In addition to taking the kinds of notes I just described, begin to read it carefully and summarize the author's major positions and how he or she has justified and presented them. Include facts that seem useful or that contradict other facts you have found. Also mark the author's insights that strike you, whether or not you agree with them. I like to make up my own source-rating scale for each research project. If I'm taking notes on my computer, I choose Wingdings like smiley faces or a bull's eye, using a symbol, meaningful only to me, to register my opinion about each source, or to show how I might use it. If I'm reading a printout or photocopy I am going to keep, then I just highlight key ideas and make notes in the margins.

Evaluation: How?

What are the criteria to use for evaluating a source? It would be nice if there were a universal, official list you could memorize in childhood, like multiplication tables or spelling rules, to apply automatically to sources for the rest of your research life. Such a list doesn't exist, but somewhere on almost every college's Web site—probably under the library category and several links down—is a document that makes a stab at it. You can most easily find it by searching the site using the terms *evaluate* and *source.* Typically the criteria offered will range from superficial characteristics anyone can determine about a source to esoteric ones only an experienced researcher can appreciate. For instance, most of these Web pages say that a source is "better" than another for use in an academic argument if

a. It was published recently
b. Its author is an established scholar
c. It was published by an academic publisher (if a book)
d. It was published by a peer-reviewed journal (if an article)
e. It has extensive notes and/or bibliography
f. It has been favorably reviewed or influenced later work

But how is a novice supposed to figure out anything other than how current a source is and whether it points to other sources? I think it is absurd—not to mention frustrating—for you to apply these criteria on your own. Instead, **the wise way to evaluate sources when you are new to a field or topic is to relate each item you are considering to your research question, keeping in mind the types of relevant sources you imagined when you brainstormed.** A source will also be valuable if it helps you with background information or provides fruitful keywords. If the source gives its author's credentials, has been published by a university press (or has a *.edu* suffix if it is a Web site), is referred to by several other sources you are reading, or just seems to reek of erudition, take that as a positive sign. Always keep in mind, however, that if you don't understand a source, or can't relate it to your research question, then it is useless for your work.

When you are doing your first or second research project in an area, you will probably not be able to make all these assessments on your own, so I urge you to discuss the sources you identify with your instructor as early in the process as possible, then apply the guidelines you learn to your future judgments. Here is a chart that discusses the basic evaluation criteria, with some important advice at the end.

Factor	Reasoning
Date of the source	For primary sources, you should be looking for evidence that appeared at or near the time of the event you are studying. Keep in mind that important primary sources are often reprinted, collected together in an anthology, or edited by experts. This does not change their nature—they are still primary—but it

Factor	Reasoning
Date of the source	does change their publication date. Hence, it is important to notice the creation date as well as the publication date of any source you are considering. The item itself should make this clear on the copyright page, in an introduction, or in a note. When in doubt, a reference librarian can help you. For secondary, especially scholarly, sources, the more recent something is, the more helpful it is likely to be because the author will have drawn on earlier evidence.
Author's credentials	You should be interested not just in someone's academic degrees but in the totality of their experience prior to producing the source you want to use. The question you want to ask yourself is, what makes (or would have made) this person an expert on my topic? It helps if you recognize their affiliation, often listed somewhere within a book or at the bottom of the first page of a scholarly journal article, but don't use that factor to exclude freelancers or writers whose institutions you have never heard of. Again, a reference librarian can help you determine what else an author has written and their career path.
Sponsor's reputation and intent	This refers to book, periodical, and newspaper publishers, and to funding organizations, such as the National Science Foundation or an oil company. Issues include whether the sources they publish have been refereed by outside experts before publication and whether the sponsor has a hidden

(continued)

Factor	Reasoning
Sponsor's reputation and intent	agenda or particular social or political bent. Usually the "about us" statement on the sponsor's Web site will provide their mission and background information. You should not automatically reject "iffy" sources, but instead acknowledge their origin in your own argument.
Leads	When you examine any source (other than a work of fiction), be sure to notice its own documentation. Ask yourself whether its notes and list of works cited are likely to point you to other useful sources, and whether it provides tables, photographs, maps, or other features that relate to your topic.

If a source seems crucial, but all you have seen is its table of contents, another writer's mention, or an abstract (summary) in a database, *and* if the source is not readily available at your library, discuss your evidence with your professor or a reference librarian. They will help you decide whether the source is likely to add significantly to your argument. If so, you can decide whether it is worth the effort and wait to obtain it.

If you have in hand a source that you know is crucial to your argument but you want expert opinion on it, you can search for reviews (if it's a book), or you can search for responses to it in later articles (if it's a scholarly or popular, but controversial, article). Confer with a reference librarian about how do these things, but be sure to take along all the details you have. The same is true if you are focusing on a historical event or person and would like to identify contemporary or subsequent views.

Seek Advice

At least once while you are still in the scouting-and-trapping mode, I urge you to discuss the sources you have identified with your professor and a librarian. This step is essential if someone recommends a source but you are not sure why it would help you. Visit during your instructor's office hours, drop by the reference desk when it's not busy, make brief appointments: whatever it takes to show these seasoned researchers what you have discovered and get their input on the merit of each source. This is not a good time to use e-mail or instant messaging, even if that is the regular way you communicate with faculty and librarians, because they need to see everything you are considering. If you are in a small class, ask your teacher to set aside part of a session as a group workshop, a kind of adult show-and-tell, during which students can each present the sources they have located so far and get reactions from one another.

I also encourage you to tell your instructor and a librarian what finding tools, especially article databases or search engines, you have already used and ask what others they would suggest. You may think you are getting feedback that is specific to your project (and of course you are), but you will also be able to extrapolate the same criteria to all your future research.

On Using Sources

If you have taken a composition or expository writing course, you probably own a textbook that treats not only the rules of grammar and punctuation but also diction (how word choice affects your argument) and bibliographic style (how to document your sources). If you do not have such a handbook, then I suggest you buy a used copy from a traditional or online bookstore or at a local book sale. Like a collegiate dictionary and a good thesaurus, a guide to writing will serve you well for years to come, and I have listed a few standard ones in the bibliography.

There are as many ways to use sources as there are researchers who discover them. Sources can summarize previous work, offer a fact, validate a method, justify a finding, or clarify a point. They can provide framework, direction, vocabulary, or connections. Just remember that in serious writing, **sources precede and support an argument, not vice versa.** (Only debaters, marketers, lobbyists, and politicians can get away with making a claim and then selecting just the sources that "prove" it.) If you are working from a preconceived opinion, rather than from a genuine research question, then you have matters backward.

If you can imagine how a source would enhance your argument, try it out. Then ask someone you trust whether the result is effective. If they tell you it detracts or distracts from your argument, either abandon the source or alter what you do with it.

On Not Abusing Sources

You know what plagiarism is—using someone else's ideas or words without admitting as much—and you know that it is dishonest. But let's look at the issue from other perspectives. Once you have made it through the research process, experienced an insight, spun an argument, written and presented the result of all that effort, would *you* want someone else to "borrow" your work and claim it as his or her own? Frankly, no one should get away with thought theft, whether the thoughts in question are yours or Emily Dickinson's.

Faculty have several ways to vet student research projects that they think have been plagiarized in whole or in part. A red flag goes up in any teacher's mind if the writing or citing practices in a paper are significantly different from the student's previous work. Sometimes a professor will actually recognize the origin of a passage or of the entire essay, or will discern from the context that the student read only an abstract, not the full article they cite (this is technically not plagiarism, but it is definitely deceptive). Other times, an instructor will replicate what the student has probably done, entering key terms describing the topic in a search engine or in a database containing full texts of chapters or journal articles. There are also Web-based services, like Turnitin, that for a fee will attempt to identify where a paper really came from. Not surprisingly, faculty get irritated when they suspect plagiarism. They abhor it as academic fraud and are not happy to stop what they are doing to verify their suspicion—in effect, to do research to prove that the student *didn't* do any. Professors know this is their duty and that, if they are right, they will need to confront the student immediately and become involved in an arduous administrative or judicial proceeding.

This is nasty business all around, just how nasty you should consider long before temptation strikes. Composition textbooks and writing manuals all discuss plagiarism, so if you have one, that's a good place to look for the difference between the right and the wrong use of sources. Many colleges require first-year students, as part of their orientation to campus life, to attend a session that covers plagiarism and its consequences. Some schools reinforce the message with an honor code students must sign, agreeing to follow its provisions in all their academic work. In any case, you need to read and understand your college's official statement defining plagiarism in the larger context of intellectual honesty, trust, and respect for others' work. It will give examples that distinguish between using information that is common knowledge, and hence needs no citation, and using material—ideas, discoveries, expressions, and the like—that must always be cited fully. If you misplace your copy of this document, you can find it on your institution's Web site by searching words like *plagiarism, integrity, responsibility,* or *conduct.*

When you acknowledge the contributions of others to your project, you are doing more than just demonstrating that you did your own research. You are also supporting your conclusions, so that your work cannot be attacked as unfounded or frivolous. Recall that new knowledge builds on old, and that it is impossible for someone else to appreciate the shape of your argument if you don't reveal what materials you used to construct it. Even if your insight has never occurred to another human being, you still want to present it in the context of related ideas, pointing out whose thoughts and sentences those are. When you cite sources accurately and conscientiously, your own work becomes a link to the long chain of discourse on your topic. To that end,

MARY'S MAXIM #16: WHEN IN DOUBT, DOCUMENT

Endgames

Students often ask when they can quit searching for sources and get down to writing about them. No wonder they are confused, because the end of the library research process usually overlaps the beginning of the writing process. There is no bright line between these activities and no guideline other than to keep working with your ideas and sources until insight happens and an argument emerges from the chaos. What you want to avoid, above all, is becoming paralyzed by piles of sources or the fear that insight will never come. If you halt the process, you lose energy, and perhaps also direction, both precious commodities. Writing handbooks are full of antidotes for this complaint, such as prewriting exercises that concentrate on what a specific source has to offer, or sharing a draft of your introduction with one or two other students to get their reaction. Best of all, I think, is to ask faculty and other veteran writers you meet how they cope with uncertainty in their own work.

As with any major undertaking, library research has ups and downs. On bad days I switch gears to get myself un-stuck: instead of searching yet another database when I already have plenty of sources, I might rearrange the ones I've found and skim them in chronological order from the oldest to the most recent. Just reordering evidence like this helps me spot connections and can rekindle my enthusiasm. Or I might play my own devil's advocate and pretend to be an antagonistic or skeptical reader. This scenario forces me to decide which of my sources is the most persuasive. That's the one I want as the finale of my argument, right before my conclusion. Then I reason backward about how best to lead up to it with my other sources.

Here are some other ploys you can try to keep your mind engaged with a project that seems stagnant:

- Give yourself *one* day off, but during that day talk with a friend about your project. Instead of complaining, explain what you've learned, and ask your friend to react. This is like brainstorming at the beginning of the process, only now you have something substantive to share, and your friend is serving as your first critic, in the positive sense of the word.

- Pick up any issue of *The Atlantic Monthly, The New Yorker,* or another periodical that publishes essays on a wide variety of topics. Read an article that interests you, then think about its structure and how the writer mixes ideas and evidence. The piece will probably not be a model for your own project, but just thinking about how others make their points can get you moving forward again.

- Ask your instructor to read and respond to a draft of your research paper or, if you are preparing an oral presentation, a detailed outline. (Offer to supply a short cover sheet listing the two or three issues you are most concerned about, and ask your instructor to address just those. For instance, Does my argument need an additional *type* of source, and if so, what? Does my argument lead to my conclusion, or is there a logical connection missing? How can I make the progression of my argument clearer or more interesting?) You will need this feedback several days before the final version is due so that you can reflect on it and incorporate the suggestions. If your instructor declines, don't be offended. There could be lots of valid reasons, not the least of which is equity. A teacher may not want to provide extra help to one student if she cannot do so for everyone else in the class. Instead, try to find a student specializing in the field—a graduate student or an undergraduate major—and ask for the same favor.

- Determine your own "production" style and make it work for you. Some people like to edit their own work, while others prefer to refine their writing as they go, then turn it in and be done with it. If your inclination is the former, make sure you allow enough time for revision, perhaps a half hour per page of your draft, ideally with a good night's sleep thrown in. If your approach is to polish your logic and prose en route, you will need more time for composition and may want to make use of word-processing features such as inserting comments to yourself as reminders of points to come back to, spelling and grammar checking, and using the built-in thesaurus to look for synonyms. In either case, be sure to make both a hard copy and a final computer file of what you submit.

One last observation and a suggestion: the longer the paper and the more sources you use, the more important it is to have breathing space in the process, so that you can complete a draft and let it sit for a few days before you revise it. Use the time away from writing to tidy up your list of works cited and verify any source you have used but whose citation is lacking a standard element, such as the city of publication for a book or the issue number for a journal article. Create the list in the bibliographic style you are using, so it is ready to go when your revision is.

In Conclusion

The end of your project should not be the end of your inquiry. Once your paper is done or your presentation is over—and even before you get a grade and comments back from your professor—take time to reflect on the entire process and imagine how you can improve it the next time. Ask yourself such questions as

- What kinds of reference tools gave you the best background at the start?
- How helpful were brainstorming and keeping a research log?
- Did keyword or assigned-subject searching prove more fruitful?
- To what extent were sources cited by others in fact good leads?
- How do scholars from different fields grapple with the same topic?
- Did you need to refine your argument along the way?
- What prompted your insight?
- What were the ways you finally used sources in your work?

You will learn a lot from such introspection, lessons you can apply to all your future projects. Once you master the concepts and steps of the library research process, you can transfer the experience with confidence across time, place, disciplines, and technology.

Appendix A

⤸

Good Habits, Helpful Hints, and Wrong Assumptions

GOOD

Habit 1: Discuss your project with friends throughout the process and heed their comments.

Habit 2: Rehearse your argument in your mind while you exercise and before you fall asleep.

Habit 3: Allow twice as much time for your research as you think you should need.

Habit 4: Critique your own research process both as it occurs and when it is over.

HELPFUL

Hint 1: Always have your research log handy to capture wild ideas.

Hint 2: Identify and examine more sources than you expect to use. Then you can choose the best ones to make your case.

Hint 3: Get to know older students who specialize in fields related to your project. Their reflections will be invaluable.

Hint 4: Learn the name and e-mail address of any librarian who helps you extensively. Then you will have someone to contact at the start of your future research projects.

<table>
<thead>
<tr><th colspan="2" align="center">WRONG</th></tr>
</thead>
<tbody>
<tr><td>Assumption 1:</td><td>All good sources are in English.</td></tr>
<tr><td>Assumption 2:</td><td>Everything I need is, and always will be, digital and freely available on the Web.</td></tr>
<tr><td>Assumption 3:</td><td>College writing is no different than high school writing: just analyzing and synthesizing sources and stating a conclusion.</td></tr>
<tr><td>Assumption 4:</td><td>It's OK to use someone else's idea in my work without documenting it, as long as I don't quote it exactly.</td></tr>
</tbody>
</table>

Appendix B

―――――― ⟅ ――――――

Mary's Maxims Compiled

1. IMAGINATION AND INSIGHT ARE INSEPARABLE.

2. BE SURE YOU UNDERSTAND THE ASSIGNMENT.

3. WHEN PICKING A TOPIC, LIKE IT OR LEAVE IT OR TWEAK IT.

4. NEVER REJECT A CRAZY IDEA, JUST RECORD IT.

5. PRACTICE THINKING ABOUT SOURCES.

6. THOSE WHO BAIL MAY WELL FAIL.

7. VERIFY, VERIFY, VERIFY.

8. TAKING TIME WILL SAVE TIME.

9. EXPECT COMPLEXITY.

10. EXERT MIND, MOUSE, AND MUSCLE TOGETHER.

11. ONE GOOD THING LEADS TO ANOTHER.

12. IF AT FIRST YOU DON'T SUCCEED, READ THE SEARCH TIPS.

13. DON'T SETTLE FOR WHAT'S HANDY.

14. CURIOSITY BEGETS SERENDIPITY.

15. GIVE YOUR ARGUMENT TIME TO MATURE.

16. WHEN IN DOUBT, DOCUMENT.

Appendix C

— ☙ —

Research Timelines

Here are three scenarios for a typical college research project: one assuming six weeks lead time, one assuming four weeks, and one assuming just two weeks. In each case, the clock starts the first day you begin to think about the project and ends the day you submit your paper or make your presentation. (You should also take time to reflect on the entire experience when it is over, in order to distill some wisdom from it for the future, but these models do not include that step.) These are *ideal* schedules that you can adapt to your own situation. Notice that the shorter the period, the less time you can spend at each stage and the fewer options you will have. To remove other variables, let's pretend the assignment is identical for each case. (This description is adapted from that of a joint American Studies/ Sociology course offered at Princeton University.)

This is an American Culture course with the title Immigrant America, which will review the historical and contemporary evidence of U.S.-bound international migration. It will examine the forms of economic, political, linguistic, and social adaptation of immigrant groups to the United States, with a focus on the second-generation experience, those born here whose parents came from other countries. In addition to midterm and final examinations, there will be a ten-to-

(continued on next page)

twelve-page research paper that compares one feature of two different immigrant groups living in the same area of the United States today. Guidelines for the paper are that

- Sources should include newspaper articles, periodical articles, and at least two peer-reviewed articles. Optional sources may be books, chapters of books, Web sites, interviews, demographic statistics, and primary documents produced by immigrants themselves
- The paper must develop an argument about the immigrant experience, not be merely a list of similarities and differences between the groups chosen
- The paper is due at the last class session and counts as 50 percent of the course grade

Six-Week-or-Longer Research Plan

WEEK 1

❑ Clarify the assignment, if necessary

❑ Begin a research log and start thinking about what you already know and what groups would be interesting

❑ Review your class notes; do some background reading in a subject encyclopedia on immigrants, such as the *Gale Encyclopedia of Multicultural America* (probably shelved in the library's reference room); browse both the reference collection and the stacks in the vicinity of the encyclopedia's call number (E184.A1 ... if your library uses the Library of Congress classification, or 305.8 ... if your library uses Dewey classification); experiment with keyword searching in the library's online catalog, using the names of groups you are interested in,

combined with the truncated term *immigra** (check
what the wildcard symbol is for your catalog; it might
not be an asterisk)

❑ Choose a *tentative* research topic (the two groups you
will concentrate on); write down your ideas so far; arrange with a friend or two to brainstorm

WEEK 2

❑ Conduct a brainstorming session, making detailed
notes about new angles that come up in the conversation

❑ Write a precise research question you can apply to both
immigrant groups you will study; if possible, discuss
your research question briefly with your professor to
make sure it is feasible

❑ Begin more systematic searching of the online catalog,
moving from keyword searching to determining the
actual subject headings of relevant books, then using
those links to identify additional sources; spend some
more time browsing in the stacks; skim the table of
contents, index, and bibliography of any book that
looks useful, and if it strikes you as particularly relevant,
check it out and read it thoroughly, taking detailed
notes

❑ Start compiling lists in your research log of all the steps
you take and of the relevant keywords, call numbers,
and subject headings you discover

WEEK 3

❑ Confer with a reference librarian about which article
database(s) will be best to search and about special
collections or nonbook materials (such as videos or

photographs) that may exist related to immigrants; also confer about organizations that support, or oppose, immigration and read their mission statements on their Web sites; if your brainstorming led you to statistical data or government documents as possible sources, ask the librarian about how to access those as well

❑ Search the suggested databases for newspaper articles, periodical articles, and peer-reviewed articles; if you discover articles that are not available in full text in these databases, ask how to obtain them and then do so

❑ If you intend to do any field research, such as interviewing immigrants or people who work with immigrants, make sure you follow your college's guidelines for this type of research (ask your professor); schedule a time to conduct this research and prepare for it carefully

❑ Read and take notes; start to organize the information you have discovered so far

WEEK 4

❑ Conduct your field research, if that is part of your research method; analyze the results immediately

❑ If you've already had an insight, move forward with it to write a thesis statement, outline your argument with supporting sources for each point, and begin drafting your paper; also decide what additional sources you still need and repeat the relevant steps to identify and obtain them

❑ If you have not yet had an insight, keep reading and attempt to track down some of the most interesting sources listed in the bibliographies of books you have checked out or the works cited lists in the peer-reviewed articles you have discovered; confer again with a reference librarian about how to locate a recent survey article on research related to immigration (this will tell you the most compelling issues experts are discussing and you can use one of their points as a way to view your own sources)

❑ Speak again with your professor, especially if you do not yet have an insight or are not sure whether some of your sources are reliable

WEEK 5

❑ Complete a draft of your paper and have someone else read it for clarity

❑ Compile a list of all the sources you are using to make your argument, following the bibliographic style your professor has specified (if he or she has not indicated a style, or just tells students to be complete and consistent in their works cited, then use the style known as Turabian, a full citation to which is in the bibliography of this book)

❑ Spend a day or two away from your project, so that you can look at your draft again with fresh eyes

WEEK 6

❑ Revise your draft, check for the accuracy of your quotes and notes, add your bibliography, spell-check everything, make sure your pages are numbered, and add any illustrations (for instance, a table or graph showing the change in education level or income of each of your immigrant groups over time); print out two copies of your paper, one to turn in and one to keep

❑ Submit your paper

Four-Week Research Plan

- No time for field research
- Little time to explore special collections or nonprint sources
- Minimal time for obtaining sources from other libraries
- Less time for reflection and revision

WEEK 1

❑ Clarify the assignment, if necessary

❑ Begin a research log and start thinking about what you already know and what groups would be interesting

❑ Review your class notes; do some background reading in a subject encyclopedia on immigrants, such as the *Gale Encyclopedia of Multicultural America* (probably shelved in the library's reference room); browse both the reference collection and the stacks in the vicinity of the encyclopedia's call number (E184.A1 . . . if your library uses the Library of Congress classification, or 305.8 . . . if your library uses Dewey classification); experiment with keyword searching in the library's online catalog, using the names of groups you are interested in, combined with the truncated term *immigra** (check what the wildcard symbol is for your catalog, it might not be an asterisk)

❑ Choose a *tentative* research topic (the two groups you will concentrate on); write down your ideas so far; arrange with a friend or two to brainstorm

❑ Conduct a brainstorming session, making detailed notes about new angles that come up in the conversation

❑ Write a precise research question you can apply to both immigrant groups you will study; if possible, discuss your research question briefly with your professor to make sure it is feasible

WEEK 2

❑ Begin more systematic searching of the online catalog, moving from keyword searching to determining the actual subject headings of relevant books, then using those links to identify additional sources; spend some more time browsing in the stacks; skim the table of contents, index, and bibliography of any book that looks useful, and if it strikes you as particularly relevant, check it out and read it thoroughly, taking detailed notes

❑ Start compiling lists in your research log of all the steps you take and of the relevant keywords, call numbers, and subject headings you discover

❑ Confer with a reference librarian about which article database(s) will be best to search and about special collections or nonbook materials (such as videos or photographs) that may exist related to immigrants; also confer about organizations that support, or oppose, immigration and read their mission statements on their Web sites; if your brainstorming led you to statistical data or government documents as possible sources, ask the librarian about how to access those as well

❑ Search the suggested databases for newspaper articles, periodical articles, and peer-reviewed articles; if you discover articles that are not available in full text in these databases, ask how to obtain them and then do so

❑ Read and take notes; start to organize the information you have discovered so far

WEEK 3

- ❑ If you've already had an insight, move forward with it to write a thesis statement, outline your argument with supporting sources for each point, and begin drafting your paper; also decide what additional sources you still need and repeat the relevant steps to identify and obtain them
- ❑ If you have not yet had an insight, keep reading and attempt to track down some of the most interesting sources listed in the bibliographies of books you have checked out or the works cited lists in the peer-reviewed articles you have discovered; confer again with a reference librarian about how to locate a recent survey article on research related to immigration (this will tell you the most compelling issues experts are discussing and you can use one of their points as a way to view your own sources)
- ❑ Speak again with your professor, especially if you do not yet have an insight or are not sure whether some of your sources are reliable
- ❑ Complete a draft of your paper and have someone else read it for clarity
- ❑ Compile a list of all the sources you are using to make your argument, following the bibliographic style your professor has specified (if he or she has not indicated a style, or just tells students to be complete and consistent in their works cited, then use the style known as Turabian, a full citation to which is in the bibliography of this book)

WEEK 4

- ❑ Spend a day away from your project, so that you can look at your draft again with fresh eyes

❏ Revise your draft, check for the accuracy of your quotes
and notes, add your bibliography, spell-check everything, make sure your pages are numbered, and add any
illustrations (for instance, a table or graph showing the
change in education level or income of each of your
immigrant groups over time); print out two copies of
your paper, one to turn in and one to keep

❏ Submit your paper

Two-Week-or-Less Research Plan

• No time for field research
• No time to explore special collections or nonprint sources
• No time for obtaining sources from other libraries
• Little time for brainstorming, reflection, or revision

WEEK 1

❏ Clarify the assignment, if necessary

❏ Begin a research log and start thinking about what you
already know and what groups would be interesting

❏ Review your class notes; do some background reading
in a subject encyclopedia on immigrants, such as the
Gale Encyclopedia of Multicultural America (probably
shelved in the library's reference room); browse both
the reference collection and the stacks in the vicinity of
the encyclopedia's call number (E184.A1 . . . if your library uses the Library of Congress classification, or
305.8 . . . if your library uses Dewey classification); experiment with keyword searching in the library's online
catalog, using the names of groups you are interested in,
combined with the truncated term *immigra** (check

what the wildcard symbol is for your catalog, it might not be an asterisk)

❑ Choose a *tentative* research topic (the two groups you will concentrate on); write down your ideas so far; if possible, conduct a brainstorming session with friends, making detailed notes about new angles that come up in the conversation

❑ Write a precise research question you can apply to both immigrant groups you will study; if possible, discuss your research question briefly with your professor to make sure it is feasible

❑ Begin more systematic searching of the online catalog, moving from keyword searching to determining the actual subject headings of relevant books, then using those links to identify additional sources; spend some more time browsing in the stacks; skim the table of contents, index, and bibliography of any book that looks useful, and if it strikes you as particularly relevant, check it out and read it thoroughly, taking detailed notes

❑ Start compiling lists in your research log of all the steps you take and of the relevant keywords, call numbers, and subject headings you discover

❑ Confer with a reference librarian about which article database(s) will be best to search and about organizations that support, or oppose, immigration and read their mission statements on their Web sites; if your brainstorming led you to statistical data or government documents as possible sources, ask the librarian about how to access those as well

❑ Search the suggested databases for newspaper articles, periodical articles, and peer-reviewed articles; if you discover articles that are not available in full text in these databases, ask whether and where your library has them

❑ Read and take notes; start to organize the information you have discovered so far

WEEK 2

❑ If you've already had an insight, move forward with it to write a thesis statement, outline your argument with supporting sources for each point, and begin drafting your paper; also decide what additional sources you still need and repeat the relevant steps to identify and obtain them in your library

❑ If you have not yet had an insight, keep reading and attempt to track down some of the most interesting sources listed in the bibliographies of books you have checked out or the works cited lists in the peer-reviewed articles you have discovered

❑ Speak again with your professor, especially if you do not yet have an insight or are not sure whether some of your sources are reliable

❑ Complete a draft of your paper and compile a list of all the sources you are using to make your argument, following the bibliographic style your professor has specified (if he or she has not indicated a style, or just tells students to be complete and consistent in their works cited, then use the style known as Turabian, a full citation to which is in the bibliography of this book)

❑ Revise your draft, check for the accuracy of your quotes and notes, add your bibliography, spell-check every-thing, make sure your pages are numbered, and add any illustrations (for instance, a table or graph showing the change in education level or income of each of your immigrant groups over time); print out two copies of your paper, one to turn in and one to keep

❏ Submit your paper

Appendix D

⌒

Questions to Ask Your Instructor

You will need to know the answers to these questions for every library research project you undertake. Faculty will probably cover most, if not all, of these issues via written guidelines or announcements they make in class, but if not, speak up. Do not annoy the professor, but make sure you and your classmates get the answers somehow.

1. What is the role of the research project in the context of the course?

2. Would you please clarify the [scope, criteria, stages, length, or deadlines] of the assignment?

3. What would make a good paper or presentation topic?

4. What types, format, and variety of primary and secondary sources are appropriate?

5. What bibliographic style should I follow for my notes and bibliography?

6. Can you please provide an example of an A paper in this course, or suggest a published essay that I can use as a model?

Research Appointment Worksheet

You should be able to answer most of these questions, at least in part, before you confer with either your professor or a librarian about your research. Use your conversation to help you fill in the blanks.

1. Please describe your primary source(s).

2. What context are you using to view your primary source?

3. What is your research question at this point? (If more than one, please list them all.)

4. What keywords best describe your research?

5. What academic fields are interested in your research question(s)?

6. What factual or background information do you still need?

7. What reference works, print or electronic, or online databases have you already used?

8. What kinds of additional sources would you like to find?

9. Are there any sources you have identified but have not yet been able to obtain? If so, what are they?

10. Please describe any problems or concerns you have with this research project.

Glossary of Library Research Terms

╰╮

Some of these terms do not occur in this book, but I have included them because they are likely to come up in discussions with faculty and librarians.

abstract. The summary of a researcher's argument, approach, and conclusions. Abstracts are typically written by the author of a scholarly article or dissertation, and appear as a paragraph at the beginning of the source. Most databases provide the abstract, whether or not they also link to the full text of the source. Researchers often judge the relevance of a source based solely on its abstract. See also statistical abstract.

academic argument. See argument.

academic article. See peer-reviewed article.

academic essay. See essay.

academic journal. See scholarly journal.

academic library. The library that serves students, faculty, and staff of a college or university. It may be housed in a single building or in several campus locations. See also archives; branch library; research library; special collection; special library.

access. Refers to the availability of sources. Researchers want access to information and specific sources, whether or not a library owns the actual item. A library can provide access to material it does not own by borrowing it, by obtaining a photocopy from another library, or by licensing a full-text database that includes the source. Advanced researchers may need to travel to libraries or archives to use materials on site. See also document delivery; interlibrary loan.

acquisitions. A general term for the process of selecting, ordering, and receiving materials for library collections. See also cataloging; indexing.

advanced search. One method of keyword searching in an online catalog or article database. An advanced search screen usually provides multiple boxes where the researcher can enter terms and phrases, plus a way to connect those ideas. Also called a guided search. See also Boolean logic; connectors; logic.

"Aha!" moment. See insight.

almanac. A fact tool providing a miscellaneous assortment of information and usually updated every year.

alphabetical order. Either of two ways to arrange words by their spelling: letter-by-letter, which ignores spaces between words, or word-by-word, which treats a space between words as a character coming before the letter *A*. In letter-by-letter alphabetical order, Newark comes before New York, as if the latter were spelled NewYork (that is, without a space). In word-by-word alphabetical order, New York (beginning with a shorter element followed by a space) comes before Newark (a longer word). When researchers cannot find information in reference tools, it is often because the alphabetical order is not what they expect. This glossary uses the letter-by-letter method.

annotated bibliography. A list of sources that includes a brief summary of each, which may be descriptive, critical, or both. Faculty may request that students submit an annotated bibliography during the library research process as a way to tell what sources students have discovered and how they expect to use them. Scholars sometimes publish extensive annotated bibliographies on a topic, either as long journal articles or as whole books. See also abstract; review; survey article.

anthology. A book or periodical issue containing sources that originally appeared separately in another publication. Also called a collection. See also edited volume; festschrift; proceedings.

APA style. The documentation format recommended by the American Psychological Association and used in many social science disciplines. See the bibliography of this book for a complete citation. See also bibliographic style.

archives. The sources, such as correspondence files or financial records, created by organizations or governments in the course of their operations. See also finding aid; papers; special collection.

argument. A researcher's carefully crafted exposition of an insight based on sources. Also called an academic argument. See also audience; insight; thesis statement.

article. A piece of writing shorter than a book, appearing in a newspaper, magazine, periodical, journal, or anthology. To be scholarly, an article must be based on research and include documentation of all sources. See also essay; peer-reviewed article.

article database. Any large group of articles whose descriptive records or full texts can be retrieved via the accompanying search feature. An article database may be multidisciplinary or specific to a discipline and is usually licensed to libraries for a fee by the company that creates and maintains it. Often called just a database. See also article; Boolean logic; database; hits; limiting.

assigned-subject searching. See concept searching; descriptors; keyword searching; known-item searching; subject headings; subject searching; thesaurus.

atlas. An assortment of maps published in book format and often containing other geographical information as well.

audience. The readers a writer intends to reach with an article or a book, or the people a speaker makes a presentation to.

author-date citation. The documentation format that places the author and year of a source immediately following its mention in an argument, then provides the full reference at the end of the text. See also APA style; bibliographic style; Chicago style; CSE style; in-text citation; MLA style; Turabian.

background. Factual information on a broad subject, necessary for determining what aspects of it could become an interesting, feasible research topic. Hybrid reference tools, such as encyclopedias, provide reliable background at the start of a research project.

barcode. A unique number sequence printed on a small label and used by libraries to keep track of volumes in their collection. Borrowers' cards also have barcodes, allowing a library's electronic circulation system to pair the item with the user. See also circulation.

bibliographic description. The basic facts about a source—such as author, title, and year of publication—expressed in a standard format and coded so that the item can be found via an online catalog or database search.

bibliographic essay. See survey article.

bibliographic style. Any standardized format for citing the sources used in a research project. See also APA style; bibliography; Chicago style; CSE style; documentation; endnotes; footnotes; in-text citation; MLA style; Turabian.

bibliography. A finding tool that lists the sources consulted or used by a researcher. The other major types of finding tools are catalogs and indexes. Also called works cited. See also APA style; Chicago style; CSE style; MLA style; Turabian.

biographical compendium. A fact tool with entries for individuals, sometimes limited by their nationality, occupation, or whether they are living or deceased. If it also provides a list of works by or about each person, then it functions as a hybrid tool. Also called a biographical dictionary, biographical directory, or biographical encyclopedia.

book. A print publication with its own title and that is fifty pages or longer. See also anthology; monograph; pamphlet; reference work.

Boolean logic. The usual way to combine concepts when seeking sources in an online catalog or article database. Boolean logic allows the researcher to group similar aspects of a topic and relate them using the terms *and* (to narrow a search), *or* (to broaden a search), or *not* (to exclude a factor). See also advanced search; connectors; logic; Venn diagram.

bound volumes. Issues of a periodical or other serial that are physically sewn together, have hard covers, and are housed in a library's stacks, arranged by call number or title. Bound volumes include the consecutive issues from earlier years, whereas current issues may be kept on racks in a separate area or reading room to make browsing easier. Older newspaper issues, as well as back issues of many periodicals and scholarly journals, are likely to be available in digital form or in microform, something a library's online catalog will make clear. See also holdings.

branch library. A library on a college or university campus, often serving primarily undergraduates or students and faculty in a particular discipline, such as the life sciences or music. See also academic library; research library; special library.

browse. The activity of looking at adjacent books on the same shelf or articles within the same periodical. Browsing can also be done in many online catalogs and article indexes by skimming the titles, subject terms, tables of contents, or abstracts of items that appear in search results.

call number. A numeric or alphanumeric designation allowing books on related subjects to be shelved near one another.

See also browse; classification; Dewey classification; Library of Congress classification; stacks.

catalog. A finding tool that identifies the books, serials, and other types of sources in a library's collection. Also spelled catalogue. The other major types of finding tools are bibliographies and indexes. See also online catalog; opac.

cataloging. The process of analyzing a source so that researchers can identify it in a library's online catalog by searching for it as a known item, using keywords, or entering assigned-subject terms. See also catalog; indexing; online catalog; opac.

CBE style. See CSE style.

chapter. A distinct part of a book with its own topic and title and that is listed in the table of contents. If the book is an anthology, festschrift, or proceedings of a conference, then each chapter will be by a different author. See also edited volume.

Chicago style. The documentation format specified by *The Chicago Manual of Style* and used in books intended for both general readers and specialists. The version for academic essays and articles is by Kate Turabian. See the bibliography of this book for a complete citation. Also called either CMOS or CMS. See also bibliographic style; Turabian.

chronology. A fact tool that arranges events in the order they took place.

circulation. The unit responsible for keeping track of materials in a library's general collection, including charging books out to users, looking for lost items, reshelving returned volumes, and similar functions. See also barcode.

citation. A succinct description of a source, sufficient for another researcher to find it. Also called a reference.

classification. Any scheme for organizing concepts or physical objects, such as books. Most American libraries use either the Dewey or the Library of Congress classification system, but there are also unique ones still in use, especially in large research or special libraries. See also browse; call number; Dewey classification; Library of Congress classification.

CMOS. See Chicago style; Turabian.

CMS. See Chicago style; Turabian.

collection. (a) A library's or archives' holdings, either in total or a specific part. (b) A published work containing contributions on different topics or by different authors. See also anthology; edited volume; festschrift; proceedings.

companion. See handbook.

concept searching. The technique for identifying sources using a researcher's own terminology (keyword searching) or phrases that have already been assigned by others (subject searching). See also descriptors; subject headings; thesaurus.

concordance. A fact tool listing the vocabulary used in a specific work or group of works, and that provides the context where each word appears.

connectors. The terms used to combine concepts in a search. Also called operators. See also advanced search; Boolean logic; logic; Venn diagram.

controlled vocabulary. See descriptors; subject headings; thesaurus.

cross-reference. A pointer, often indicated by the words *See* or *See also,* to alternative or synonymous terms. See also descriptors; subject headings; thesaurus.

CSE style. The documentation format specified by the Council of Science Editors and used in many science disciplines. See the bibliography of this book for a complete citation. Also called CBE style, after its earlier name (Council of Biology Editors). See also bibliographic style.

data. Information expressed in numeric form. See also statistical abstract.

database. An electronic finding tool that may include any combination of factual information, records describing sources, or digitized sources in their entirety. A database is usually searchable by keywords, descriptors, or other characteristics such as date or language. See also article database; index.

depository. Any library that automatically receives the official publications of a government body, or of certain agencies within it, with the commitment to make these sources available to anyone. Examples are depositories for U.S. federal publications, state documents, and United Nations materials. Also called a document depository. See also government document.

descriptors. The standardized words and phrases assigned to articles in a database or index. See also concept searching; keywords; subject headings; thesaurus.

Dewey classification. A system of arranging books using three-digit numbers followed by a decimal point and additional numerals to denote aspects of a topic. Dewey classification is widely used by school and public libraries in the United States, and by some academic and large research libraries. See also browse; call number; classification; Library of Congress classification.

dictionary. A fact tool that defines all, or some subset, of the words in a language, or of words that pertain to a certain discipline. It may have other features as well, such as pronunciation, word origins, and examples of actual usage. It is usually in alphabetical order. Also called a glossary or lexicon.

digital format. Any electronically processed text or image. See also microform; print.

directory. A fact tool that identifies businesses, institutions, associations, governments, or any other organization someone may want to contact. See also biographical compendium.

disciplines. Areas of study and research. Also called fields.

display. The view of search results provided by an online catalog or article database. The researcher can usually specify how much detail to see about each source by using a menu or link, or by setting a preference.

dissertation. An apprentice monograph, based on extensive research, required for the doctoral degree by most universities. See also thesis.

document. Common term for written evidence. It is a synonym for source in many contexts. See also depository; government document. As a verb, to indicate the sources used for research.

documentary edition. A scholarly publication, often a set of many volumes, that reproduces primary sources—such as a famous person's correspondence—with extensive explanatory notes written by experts.

documentation. The notes and bibliography provided by researchers to support their own work. See also bibliographic style; bibliography; endnotes; footnotes.

document delivery. A service provided by most libraries to obtain digital copies or photocopies of journal articles that are not in their own collection. See also access; interlibrary loan.

document depository. See depository.

edited volume. A book with texts by one or more authors that has been carefully checked by an expert for accuracy. The expert will also choose among variant wordings if the texts have been previously published. See also anthology; documentary edition; festschrift; proceedings.

editor. Someone who prepares a text for publication.

editorial. A short opinion piece appearing in a newspaper or other serial publication.

e-journal. The general term for any serial publication that exists in digital format.

encyclopedia. A hybrid tool with entries that summarize knowledge on a topic and list several significant sources about it. Encyclopedias can be either general or specialized in scope. See also subject encyclopedia.

endnotes. The documentation for each point in a researcher's argument, numbered and appearing together at the end of the article, chapter, or volume. See also footnotes.

entry. The way a source is best described, usually by its title or its author's last name.

essay. A relatively short piece of expository writing built around an insight. Essays written for college courses usually involve library research and the discovery, evaluation, and incorporation of sources into an argument. See also article; peer-reviewed article.

expository writing. A type of nonfiction prose that unfolds an argument and is usually based on sources.

facsimile. The reproduction of a source that is made to look identical to the original, but that has its origin indicated at the front or back of the volume so that a researcher will know it is not counterfeit. See also reprint.

fact tool. A reference work, whether electronic or print, that provides background information on a field or topic. Examples of fact tools are almanacs, directories, and handbooks, but there are many other types. Fact tools are one of the three major categories of reference works, the others being finding tools and hybrid tools.

festschrift. A collection of specially written articles by different scholars, published to honor a prominent person or a significant event. A festschrift usually appears in book format but can also be a special issue of a journal. See also edited volume.

fields. See disciplines.

find. A verb meaning, depending on the context, to discover background information, to identify sources, to determine where sources are located, and to obtain sources.

finding aid. Detailed description of the contents of a manuscript collection or an archive.

finding tool. A reference work, whether electronic or print, that identifies sources about a field or topic. Examples of finding tools include catalogs, indexes, and bibliographies. Finding tools are one of the three major categories of reference works, the others being fact tools and hybrid tools. See also tertiary source.

focus. See insight.

focusing. See limiting.

footnotes. The documentation for each point in a researcher's argument, numbered and appearing at the bottom of each page. See also endnotes.

format. The physical aspect of a tool or source. See also digital format; microform; print.

full-text database. See database.

gazetteer. A fact tool listing places, usually in a single alphabetical order or organized by country, with a brief description of their location and significance.

general collection. The books, journals, and other print materials in a library, available to any qualified user. See also special collection.

glossary. See dictionary.

government document. Any source produced for or issued by a ruling organization. Also called an official publication. See also depository.

guide. See handbook.

guided search. See advanced search.

handbook. A fact tool that compiles all sorts of background and practical information about some field or large topic. Also called a companion, guide, or manual.

hits. The records retrieved from an online catalog or article database search. The number of hits resulting from a search can usually be reduced or increased by entering different criteria. See Boolean logic; limiting.

holdings. Information, provided by the online catalog, regarding what volumes of a multivolume set, what years of a serial, or how many copies of a book the library owns. See also record.

hybrid tool. A reference work, whether electronic or print, that provides both background information about a topic and a list of highly regarded sources. The premier example of a hybrid tool is an encyclopedia. Hybrid tools are one of the three major categories of reference works, the others being fact tools and finding tools.

ILL. The abbreviation for interlibrary loan.

imprint. The basic publication information for a book, consisting of city, publisher's name, and year.

index. A finding tool that identifies specific articles, usually providing approaches by author, assigned-subject descriptors, and keywords. The other major types of finding tools are bibliographies and catalogs. See also article database.

indexing. The process of analyzing a source so that researchers can identify it in an article database by searching for it as a known item, by using keywords, or by entering assigned-subject terms. See also article database; cataloging; descriptors; index; thesaurus.

information. The facts and ideas conveyed via any medium from one person to another.

inquiry. The term for any type of planned research, whether quantitative, qualitative, or speculative. Inquiry always relies to some extent on sources.

insight. A researcher's own idea or answer to a research question, based on sources and reflection. Insight occurs at an unpredictable point in the research process and leads to the formulation of a thesis statement and argument. Also called an "Aha!" moment or focus.

interlibrary loan. A service provided by most libraries to borrow materials that are not in their own collections, and to lend materials to other libraries. Also called ILL. See also access; document delivery.

in-text citation. The documentation format that inserts a brief parenthetical note into a sentence, with the complete citation given at the end of the essay. See also author-date citation; APA style; bibliographic style; Chicago style; CSE style; MLA style; Turabian.

investigation. Any type of inquiry in which the researcher designs and conducts a study according to standard guidelines appropriate to the topic, such as scientific method.

issue. (a) A distinct part of a continuing publication, designated by number, season, or date. (b) A controversial matter that a researcher addresses in an argument. See also serial.

journal. A serial publication containing, among other types of sources, articles by experts in a field discussing their research and insights and providing extensive documentation. The adjectives *academic, peer-reviewed, refereed,* or *scholarly* are often used to indicate the nature of a journal. See also magazine; newsmagazine; peer-reviewed article; periodical; review; scholarly journal; serial.

juried article. See peer-reviewed article.

juried journal. See scholarly journal.

keywords. A researcher's own terms or phrases to describe a topic. See also descriptors; subject headings.

keyword searching. In online catalogs or article databases, the method of entering concepts using natural language to identify relevant sources. See also Boolean logic; concept searching; connectors; subject searching; truncation; Venn diagram.

known-item searching. In online catalogs or article databases, the method of using information the researcher already has about a specific source, typically the author's name or the title. See also verification.

LC. The abbreviation for Library of Congress.

lexicon. See dictionary.

Library of Congress. The largest research library in the United States, located in three buildings next to the Capitol in Washington, DC. Commonly known by its initials, LC. See also Library of Congress classification; Library of Congress subject headings.

Library of Congress classification. An alphanumeric arrangement of books based on their content, permitting researchers to browse the shelves. Each item's call number consists of one or more capital letters followed by a whole number of up to four digits, then by one or more elements preceded by decimal points. Library of Congress classification is widely used by large libraries in the United States. See also browse; call number; classification; Dewey classification; Library of Congress.

Library of Congress subject headings. The uniform terminology used to describe the topics of books and other sources included in an online catalog. The scheme allows researchers to determine broader and narrower concepts and to move from a synonym to the standardized term. See also browse; concept searching; descriptors; Library of Congress; subject headings; subject searching; thesaurus.

library privileges. The arrangements a visiting researcher may need to make in order to use the collection of another library or archival collection.

limiting. Improving search results in an online catalog or article database by adding or deleting search criteria. Also called focusing, modifying, narrowing, qualifying, refining, or restricting. See also Boolean logic.

literature. The previous scholarly work on a research topic. See also review; survey article.

literature review. See review; survey article.

locate. To determine where a given source is, usually meaning the libraries or archives that own it. See also WorldCat.

logic. The method of reasoning a researcher uses to combine concepts or search criteria. See also advanced search; Boolean logic; connectors; Venn diagram.

magazine. A serial publication that contains news stories, opinion pieces, and feature articles on topics of general interest. Magazines are extremely useful for research in many fields, providing background and current views, but are not regarded as scholarly. They are sold via subscription and at newsstands. See also journal; newsmagazine; periodical; serial.

manual. See handbook.

manuscript. Any handwritten source. More generally, an unpublished source, existing in a special or archival collection, or privately owned. See also finding aid; special collection; typescript.

microform. The overall term for any source reproduced in miniature and requiring magnification to read. The most common types of microform are microfilm, usually 35 mm and wound on reels, and microfiche, produced on flat pieces of film. There is also a type on cardboard-like sheets, called microprint. All of these formats require readers to enlarge the type, and other special machines to print or optically scan the tiny text and images. Most libraries have a dedicated unit to house microforms and the necessary equipment to use them, with staff available to assist researchers. Although some major collections of sources, previously available only in microformat, are now being commercially digitized, it is unlikely that the format will disappear altogether in the coming decades. See also digital format; print.

MLA style. The documentation format recommended by the Modern Language Association of America and commonly used in the humanities. See the bibliography of this book for a complete citation. See also bibliographic style.

modifying. See limiting.

monograph. A book-length treatment of a topic issued by a trade or scholarly publisher, following an editorial review.

narrowing. See limiting.

newsmagazine. A type of weekly periodical that focuses on current events and topics. See also journal; magazine; periodical; serial.

news media. Any method of transmitting news and commentary about current events. Depending on the research question being investigated, news media can serve as either primary or secondary sources. See also primary source; secondary source.

newspaper. A daily or weekly serial publication aimed at the general public or at a particular audience. See also primary source; secondary source.

number. See issue.

OCLC. The Online Computer Library Center, a consortium that sponsors a unified catalog including the holdings of thousands of libraries (WorldCat), and that provides other services to support collection development, cataloging, and research. See WorldCat.

official publication. See government document.

online catalog. A finding tool describing the books, serials, videos, and other types of sources available in a given library or group of libraries. Online catalogs do *not* include articles, for which a researcher needs to search an article database or index appropriate for the topic. An online catalog may have a locally descriptive name. Also called an opac. See also union catalog; WorldCat.

opac. The acronym for online public access catalog. See online catalog.

operators. See connectors.

original material. A phrase referring to a primary source in its "raw" state. When researchers work with original material, they are touching the actual object or artifact someone used to record an event or idea, whether yesterday or centuries ago. Because these sources are unique and valuable by definition, and are often fragile, researchers need to use them in secure rooms, under supervision, and following stringent guidelines. See also archives; facsimile; manuscript; rare book; reprint; special collection; typescript.

outline. The structure of an argument.

pamphlet. A print publication with its own title and that has fewer than fifty pages. See also book.

papers. A collection of sources, such as letters, originally created and owned by an individual or a family. See also archives; finding aid; special collection.

patrons. See users.

PDA. Acronym for personal digital assistant, an electronic hand-held device that allows someone to take notes and organize information.

peer-reviewed article. An essay-length contribution written by one or more specialists, based on their research and providing documentation of their sources. The essential characteristic of such an article is that it is evaluated and approved, often anonymously, by experts in the field *prior* to publication. Also called an academic article, juried article, refereed article, or scholarly article.

peer-reviewed journal. See scholarly journal.

periodical. The most common term for a serial publication that includes articles of various lengths and types appealing to the general reader. Periodical articles are extremely useful for research in many fields, but are not regarded as scholarly—although the contributors may be scholars—because they are not peer-reviewed and do not include extensive documentation of sources. Periodicals are excellent places to find criticism of books, films, and significant developments in the visual and performing arts. Issues are usually sold via subscription and at newsstands. See also journal; magazine; newsmagazine; serial.

periodical index. See article database; index.

plagiarism. Taking someone else's work or ideas and using them as one's own, without acknowledgment. This is a form of lying and is intellectually dishonest.

plot overview. A fact tool that summarizes the characters and action in works of literature, usually novels, plays, and long poems.

primary source. Evidence produced as close as possible in time or place to an event, individual, or phenomenon. Most primary sources kept in libraries are written accounts or images made by participants, witnesses, investigators, journalists, and people in similar roles. A primary source can also be anything recorded by researchers, such as laboratory measurements or tape-recorded field notes, that represents what they studied and that can be transmitted to other people. The researcher's questions determine the nature of a given source, whether primary or secondary, for a specific project. See also secondary source; source; tertiary source.

print. The traditional format for materials held in libraries. See also digital format; microform.

privileges. See library privileges.

proceedings. The texts of presentations delivered by speakers at a scholarly meeting. Proceedings are usually published as a collection at a later date in a separate volume. Also called transactions. See also anthology; edited volume.

qualifying. See limiting.

quotation book. A fact tool that provides well-known or pithy sayings and attributes them to a written or spoken source. It may be arranged by person, date, theme, or keywords.

rare book. A print source that has a special significance beyond its content. Books and other materials can be rare for many reasons which have little or nothing to do with their market value, such as their association with a certain individual or event. See also special collection.

record. (a) Any descriptive summary of a source, such as entries found in an online catalog or article database. (b) A synonym for evidence or source. See also holdings.

refereed article. See peer-reviewed article.

refereed journal. See scholarly journal.

reference. See citation.

reference librarian. A professional who works closely with researchers to help them discover the most appropriate tools for their projects and to identify and obtain relevant sources.

reference work. Any systematically organized compilation of information useful to a researcher. See also fact tool; finding tool; hybrid tool.

refining. See limiting.

report. (a) The summary of a researcher's findings. (b) A kind of source resulting from an official investigation carried out by a government or an organization.

reprint. The reproduction of a source to make it more widely available. If it is intentionally made to resemble the original, it is called a facsimile reprint.

research library. A large library serving the needs of advanced students and scholars. Most research libraries are on university campuses, but there are national and public research libraries as well. See also academic library; special library.

research log. A step-by-step account of the process of identifying, obtaining, and evaluating sources for a specific project. Similar to a lab notebook in an experimental setting.

research question. The interesting problem that a researcher decides to address about a topic.

research review. See review; survey article.

restricting. See limiting.

results. See hits.

review. (a) A critical assessment of a source, such as a book, film, art exhibition, or performance. (b) A survey of prior research or current thinking on a topic. (c) A synonym for journal in the titles of many scholarly publications. See also abstract; annotated bibliography; survey article.

scholar. An expert in a field or on a topic, usually someone with an advanced degree and whose career centers on research, teaching, and writing for publication.

scholarly article. See peer-reviewed article.

scholarly journal. A serial publication edited by and aimed at scholars, and that principally contains peer-reviewed articles. It may also publish reports of new research, book reviews, and state-of-the-art essays. Also called an academic journal, juried journal, peer-reviewed journal, or refereed journal.

scholarly publisher. A publisher specializing in monographs and other kinds of books written by academics. See also university press.

search. Any action taken by a researcher to discover relevant background or sources. A search often involves the use of electronic finding tools such as online catalogs and article databases, but it may require print tools as well.

search strategy. A multistep plan a researcher employs to identify sources.

search tactic. A specific action a researcher takes to discover information or sources.

secondary source. The interpretation by anyone of evidence related to the event, individual, or issue under study. Most secondary sources housed in a library will be books or articles written by scholars or others familiar with the topic. The researcher's questions determine the nature of a given source, whether primary or secondary, for a specific project. Researchers, including students, are creating secondary sources every time they share an insight in the form of an argument. See also primary source; source; tertiary source.

serial. A continuing publication that can be purchased via subscription, including newspapers, magazines, newsmagazines, periodicals, journals, and other materials that appear regularly.

series. A singular noun referring to books on related topics issued by the same publisher. A series will have its own overall title, and each individual volume will be numbered in sequence.

set. All the parts of a multivolume work, such as an encyclopedia.

source. (a) In general, a tangible object containing information of any sort in any format. (b) Any evidence a researcher uses to substantiate an argument. See also bibliographic style; documentation; endnotes; footnotes; primary source; secondary source; tertiary source; tool.

special collection. Any group of materials that is housed separately in an academic or research library and that may require advance arrangements for access. Special collections typically exist for rare books, manuscripts, the archives of an organization, or works by a major author or about a narrow topic. Sometimes a library itself will create a special collection, but more often one is assembled by a connoisseur who then donates or sells it to a library. See also general collection; special library.

special issue. A number of a scholarly journal in which all the articles relate to the same topic. See also festschrift.

specialized encyclopedia. See subject encyclopedia.

special library. A collection serving researchers who have very focused information needs, such as lawyers in a firm, scientists in a laboratory, or medical personnel in a hospital. Special libraries also exist at universities to support research and teaching in certain disciplines such as agriculture or art history. See also branch library.

stacks. Shelves in a library where books and bound journal volumes are arranged, usually in call number order to permit researchers to browse. See also classification; Dewey classification; Library of Congress classification.

standing order. An arrangement a library has with a publisher to automatically acquire new books that meet certain criteria.

statistical abstract. A fact tool that compiles numeric information about a country. See also abstract; data.

statistics. The data that result from a quantitative study and have been analyzed by researchers.

storage. A location where lesser-used library materials are housed to make space in the stacks for new sources. Researchers can obtain items from storage by completing a request form.

strategy. See search strategy.

study. Research conducted according to a formal methodology appropriate to the discipline and topic. When an advanced researcher conducts a study, the usual result is a dissertation, scholarly article, or monograph.

style manual. A fact tool that describes a standard format for documenting sources in notes and bibliographies. See also APA style; bibliographic style; bibliography; Chicago style; CSE style; documentation; endnotes; footnotes; in-text citation; MLA style; Turabian.

subject encyclopedia. A reference work focused not on all knowledge but on a single discipline or broad interdisciplinary area. Extremely helpful for background information at the start of the library research process. Also called a specialized encyclopedia. See also hybrid tool.

subject headings. The standardized words or phrases assigned to a source to indicate its most significant content. Researchers can either consult each tool's own thesaurus to determine these terms, or perform a keyword search, then make use of the subject headings or descriptors assigned to relevant items in order to identify similar sources. See also descriptors; Library of Congress subject headings; thesaurus.

subject searching. In online catalogs or article databases, the method of entering concepts using subject headings or descriptors to identify sources. See also concept searching; descriptors; keyword searching; subject headings; thesaurus.

subscription. An arrangement for acquiring newspapers, periodicals, and other types of serials automatically by paying in advance.

subtitle. The secondary name of a book or journal, often preceded by a colon. A subtitle is useful for distinguishing among publications with identical or similar main titles. See also title.

survey article. An overview of previous research on a topic, often with commentary by an expert. This is an extremely helpful type of finding tool, especially at the beginning of the research process. Regular volumes of survey articles exist in many fields, typically with titles beginning with the phrases *Advances in*, *Annual Review of*, *Trends in*, or *Review of Research on*. Also called a bibliographic essay or literature review. See also abstract; annotated bibliography; review.

table of contents. A list of the major parts of a book or journal issue, giving their titles and beginning pages.

tactic. See search tactic.

tertiary source. A term scholars sometimes use for a reference work intended to help a researcher identify primary and secondary sources. See also finding tool; primary source; secondary source; source.

thesaurus. (a) Any fact tool that provides synonyms. (b) In the library research process, a list of subject headings or descriptors that researchers consult when they want to do subject searching of an online catalog or article database. A link to each tool's thesaurus usually appears at the top of a search screen or next to a search box. See also descriptors; Library of Congress subject headings; subject headings; subject searching.

thesis. A written report of a research study, submitted as a requirement for an undergraduate honors or masters degree. See also dissertation.

thesis statement. A researcher's own idea about a topic, based on insight derived from sources and reflection. A thesis statement forms the core of an argument intended to persuade an audience. See also argument; audience; insight; source.

title. (a) The name given to a tool or source by its author or publisher. (b) Word used to refer to an entire work. See also subtitle.

tool. A reference work or other container of information that a researcher consults for facts or background or to identify sources, but does not read from beginning to end. See also fact tool; finding tool; hybrid tool; source.

topic. The general concern of a research project.

trade publisher. A publisher of popular or scholarly books that are usually sold in retail bookstores.

transactions. See proceedings.

truncation. The practice of including a symbol in a keyword search to retrieve results containing any form of a term (singular, plural, and possessive, for example). The most common truncation symbol is the asterisk (*), but researchers should read each catalog's or database's help file to learn its specific options. Also called a wildcard. See also Boolean logic; connectors; keyword searching.

Turabian. The version of *The Chicago Manual of Style* intended for students and for authors of academic essays and articles. Named for its original author, Kate Turabian (1893–1987). See the bibliography of this book for a complete citation. See also bibliographic style; Chicago style.

typescript. An unpublished source created using a typewriter or word-processing software. See also manuscript.

union catalog. A composite catalog that identifies sources held by several or many libraries. See also WorldCat.

university press. A scholarly publisher of monographs, reference works, and journals, sponsored in part by one or more academic institutions. See also scholarly publisher.

users. The general term for people who take advantage of a library's collections and services. Also called patrons.

Venn diagram. The depiction of a researcher's search logic using circles to represent concepts and proximity to represent relationships. See also Boolean logic; connectors; keyword searching.

verification. The process of double-checking a citation because the original information a researcher has is incomplete or inconsistent. See also known-item searching.

volume. The physical format of a printed source, whether a book or a group of issues from the same periodical. See also bound volumes.

wildcard. See truncation.

works cited. See bibliography.

WorldCat. The online union catalog of OCLC, the largest library consortium in the world. WorldCat includes over 105 million records contributed by libraries of all types in many countries. See also locate; OCLC.

Selected Bibliography

Books Emphasizing Library Research

These are books I highly recommend. They treat many of the topics and issues I discuss, but from different angles.

Ballenger, Bruce. *The Curious Researcher: A Guide to Writing Research Papers.* 5th ed. New York: Pearson Longman, 2007.

Barzun, Jacques, and Henry F. Graff. *The Modern Researcher.* 6th ed. Belmont, CA: Thomson Wadsworth, 2004.

Booth, Wayne C., Gregory G. Colomb, and Joseph M. Williams. *The Craft of Research.* 3rd ed. Chicago: University of Chicago Press, 2008.

Kuhlthau, Carol Collier. *Seeking Meaning: A Process Approach to Library and Information Services.* 2nd ed. Westport, CT: Libraries Unlimited, 2004.

Lenburg, Jeff. *The Facts on File Guide to Research.* New York: Facts on File, 2005.

Mann, Thomas. *The Oxford Guide to Library Research.* 3rd ed. New York: Oxford University Press, 2005.

Muth, Marcia F. *Research and Writing: A Portable Guide.* Boston: Bedford/St. Martin's, 2006.

Quaratiello, Arlene Rodda. *The College Student's Research Companion.* 4th ed. New York: Neal-Schuman Publishers, 2007.

Stebbins, Leslie F. *Student Guide to Research in the Digital Age: How to Locate and Evaluate Information Sources.* Westport, CT: Libraries Unlimited, 2006.

Taylor, Terry, Joan Arth, Amy Solomon, and Naomi Williamson. *100% Information Literacy Success.* Clifton Park, NY: Thomson Delmar Learning, 2007.

Books Emphasizing College Writing

These books all do a good job of explaining how sources work in an academic essay. Most of them also serve as reference tools because they cover grammar, usage, bibliographic styles, and related topics.

Fowler, H. Ramsey, and Jane E. Aaron. *The Little, Brown Handbook.* 10th ed. New York: Pearson Longman, 2007.

Hacker, Diana. *The Bedford Handbook.* 7th ed. Boston: Bedford/St. Martin's, 2006.

Harris, Muriel, and Jennifer Kunka. *Prentice Hall Reference Guide.* 7th ed. Upper Saddle River, NJ: Prentice Hall, 2008.

Harvey, Gordon. *Writing with Sources: A Guide for Students.* Indianapolis: Hackett Publishing, 1998.

Palmquist, Mike. *The Bedford Researcher.* 2nd ed. Boston: Bedford/St. Martin's, 2006.

Spatt, Brenda. *Writing from Sources.* 7th ed. Boston: Bedford/St. Martin's, 2007.

Weidenborner, Stephen, Domenick Caruso, and Gary Parks. *Writing Research Papers: A Guide to the Process.* 7th ed. Boston: Bedford/St. Martin's, 2005.

Books about Plagiarism

These two books focus on plagiarism in an attempt to help researchers understand and avoid it.

Lipson, Charles. *Doing Honest Work in College: How to Prepare Citations, Avoid Plagiarism, and Achieve Real Academic Success.* 2nd ed. Chicago: University of Chicago Press, 2008.

Posner, Richard A. *The Little Book of Plagiarism*. New York: Pantheon Books, 2007.

Guides to Documentation

These books detail the most common rules for formatting notes and bibliographies in college essays. They also provide copious examples.

The Chicago Manual of Style. 15th ed. Chicago: University of Chicago Press, 2003. (There is also a digital version of this guide, but libraries must pay a fee to license it for their users.)

Council of Science Editors. Style Manual Committee. *Scientific Style and Format: The CSE Manual for Authors, Editors, and Publishers*. 7th ed. Reston, VA: Council of Science Editors in cooperation with the Rockefeller University Press, 2006.

Gibaldi, Joseph. *MLA Handbook for Writers of Research Papers*. 6th ed. New York: Modern Language Association of America, 2003.

Hacker, Diana, and Barbara Fister. *Research and Documentation in the Electronic Age*. 4th ed. Boston: Bedford/St. Martin's, 2006. (The Web site http://www.dianahacker.com/resdoc/ is the electronic equivalent of this book, available without restrictions.)

Publication Manual of the American Psychological Association. 5th ed. Washington, DC: American Psychological Association, 2001.

Radford, Marie L., Susan B. Barnes, and Linda R. Barr. *Web Research: Selecting, Evaluating, and Citing*. 2nd ed. Boston: Pearson/Allyn and Bacon, 2006.

Turabian, Kate L. *A Manual for Writers of Research Papers, Theses, and Dissertations: Chicago Style for Students and Researchers*. Edited by Wayne C. Booth, Gregory G. Colomb, Joseph M. Williams, and University of Chicago Press editorial staff. 7th ed. Chicago: University of Chicago Press, 2007.

Walker, Janice R., and Todd W. Taylor. *The Columbia Guide to Online Style.* 2nd ed. New York: Columbia University Press, 2006.

Index

Note: Page numbers in italics refer to definitions in the glossary.